2 ~

"In connecting to my heart I have discovered a wisdom far better than the mind chatter I took for truth most of my life. Heart consciousness is the next wave of global consciousness and is evolutionary in nature."

-Elizabeth Crow-Joong, PhD, Medical sociologist, Reiki master, and Mindfulness consultant

"Now I realize the difference between heart meditation and mindfulness meditation. I feel much more connected and a stronger sense of oneness."

-Alison Heiser, middle school teacher

"Heart consciousness adds a richer intuitive dimension to handling what life brings…a wonderful addition to the ruling mind/body brain."

-Alice Rost, Yoga Instructor

"Being present in my heart shifts my understanding of life experiences, revealing a new narrative of my life journey. Connecting with my heart has changed the way I live my life. Heart consciousness is my source of personal power, and we alter the Noosphere as we radiate love from our heart to the hearts of all beings."

-Erin Williams Bedard, Karuna Reiki master/teacher and licensed massage therapist

"Heart Centered Wellness enables me to live consciously from a state of love, honoring myself and others. I experience less fear as I trust the universe, and am empowered to offer clients a compassionate positive presence."

-Jane Brajkovich, Mental Health counselor and Arts Therapist

The Heart Field

What it is

How it works

Why it matters

Christine Bair

ISBN: 13: 978-1537022017
ISBN: 10: 1537022016

DEDICATION

To the One
who presents Love in so very many faces

TABLE OF CONTENTS

ACKNOWLEDGMENTS

Nothing is accomplished individually and myriad contributions of every kind flavor the end result. Specific thanks to my husband Richard for supporting my work in so many ways. To the Holos community, and especially Ann and Bob Nunley, for stretching me and encouraging my growth over many years. To my sister Barbara for years of gestational listening and helpful feedback. To Erin and Elizabeth who midwifed the transitional phase of this book. And to all the family, friends, teachers, students, patients, and clients who honored me with their trust in the sharing of their lives, making the One a visible reality.

The Heart Field

PART I

THE BASICS

The Heart Field

1 INTRODUCTION

If you are reading this you are probably one who asks the questions, Who am I, and why am I here? Does life have meaning and if so, how can I know what it is? Do I matter and can I make a difference in the world? For hundreds of years we in the West have tried to answer those questions by going on a mind quest. We have read books and studied with teachers, we have tried myriad techniques and used technologies reported to alter our brainwaves and frequencies. We have learned about mindfulness and been devoted to gurus. We have followed the teachings of a particular religion, tribe, or ideology. Some have provided temporary glimpses of something more, a brief experience of another way of being. Yet for the most part nothing lasting has occurred in our experience of life, our sense of ourselves. We often feel like we are working very hard but making little progress. That sense of 'not enough' keeps returning to sabotage our efforts and diminish our sense of being. How is it that so much sincere effort results in so little change? It feels so unfair that we yearn so strongly and try so hard, yet nothing seems to change.

The answer is actually simple. It is that the answers to those questions cannot be found with the mind. Our minds are a wonderful tool that use our brains to analyze information, sorting it through looking for pattern recognition, then automatically connecting us to what matches it in our previous experience, what we have been taught, the rules of life in our culture, nation, or religion. Often it is a combination of them all. This is an essential and useful function, but not one capable of addressing the questions above. Because it is the only part of our consciousness that we have been aware of, we have erroneously concluded along with scientific materialism and medical science that it is the master control and highest function of human being. If that is what we believe we continue to look for answers where they can't be found.

Our intellect is an essential aspect of our being, but it is not all of it. It is limited by its very nature in ways that make it inadequate for answering existential questions of meaning. It is the part of us that perceives ourselves as separate, our ego self. It sorts out incoming information according to past experience, but has no capability of discerning truth or untruth. Its job is to provide context for what is happening and automated reaction, but its only points of comparison are in the past. It is the active masculine principle in action; how to choose what to 'do.' Because the brain is such a vital structure in our anatomy it's easy to see how even medical science went down the path of seeing the Central Nervous System as 'control central'. It's only now as humanity observes the chaotic and often destructive results of what was intended to free and empower us that we are confronted with the stark reality that we have been looking in the wrong place for the answers to our most important life questions.

The answer has never been a secret. It has been kept alive during the centuries by mystery schools, and initiates of various cultures and spiritual teachers dedicated to passing on universal principles in the face of real threats and persecution from the dominant domains of culture, science, and religion. For those who experience life from a base of separation and 'survival of the fittest,' it makes sense that safety and security require defense and control; fear is a needed defense mechanism for survival. Since the ego self of the brain is conscious only at this level, all who do not move beyond this limited consciousness of the intellect can only perceive themselves in this way, and are thus victims of the environments that they find themselves in. Because materialism and scientism proved so materially profitable and seemed to provide fleeting security while feeding the ego self with a sense of individual importance, it became the predominant way of being that we find all around us today.

What is it that has been passed on through the centuries and been revived by master teachers at crucial points throughout history that provides us with an entirely different context for understanding life? Is it possible as we look at the state of the world today to feel any genuine sense of hope that the direction of humanity can shift? Can we ever hope to experience an ongoing inner peace and joy in day to day living and have a world of beauty, harmony, and love? I know with all my heart that the answer is an absolute YES, and unpacking the what, why, and how of that is what this book is about.

That last sentence is quite literally true. The great realization is that it is only with the heart that we are able to perceive and experience our lives, others, and the world around us from an expanded consciousness that experiences our unity and connection with all that is. We have the actual sense of the inner and outer worlds as two sides of the same thing. We know that we are body, mind, and spirit, yet little has been explained to us about how those aspects of our being are connected or able to function together as a unified whole, or how it is that they interact with each other. In our currently fragmented world we go to an MD for advice about our physical body, a counselor or psychotherapist for help with mental and emotional issues, and a priest, rabbi, pastor, imam, guru, shaman or other spiritual leader for spiritual guidance. In general we have been taught that we need an outside expert to determine our level of wellness in a particular dimension, leaving us to try to understand how all those separate aspects fit into the whole person we live our lives as. There is very little if any attention paid to how all the parts of our being interrelate and affect the others. In our dysfunctional world any aberration is pathologised and all manner of external means used to move us back into some measured range of 'normal.' We have not been taught how to access dimensions beyond the physical and mental for ourselves. While in our lives we treasure those moments when connection and joy spontaneously appear for a brief moment, they have been called 'peak experiences' as if they magically appear and quickly disappear from who knows where. When we live solely from our mind, our best understanding of wholeness and unity remains conceptual; an ideal to attain to with no practical way to attach it to our daily lives as we live them. We change our thinking and behavior but find our emotional experience remains the same. Life is unsatisfying, but we are not sure why. We tend to blame it on outside factors from relationships to jobs to where we live, the list is endless. The inner conclusion from the rational brain is that in some way we are not enough. Without other tools at our disposal we conclude that we need more information, a teacher who knows the answers, to go somewhere special, to use a technique or technology that can alter our being for us. A growing frustration and reinforced sense of inadequacy is the usual result. Many just give up and accept that life is just what they already experience. Some act out destructively toward self or others out of frustration and confusion; a deep sense of life being unfair without any real definition of what fair would look like. For others though, the inner desire and yearning for a life that is more fulfilling, more joyful, more connected, more meaningful continues to provide impetus for the search for what is true. This book is for you.

First let's update the basics of our understanding of our nature as whole beings and how the different planes of our existence relate and connect. Translating abstract scientific discoveries and spiritual principles into everyday language provides the basics of our physical, mental, emotional, and spiritual being, and a holistic and practical frame of reference with which to live more effectively from a higher level of conscious understanding. The Heart Field will be defined and demonstrated to be the central power of the vibrational essence of our human being. In particular the role of feelings and emotions is often greatly misunderstood, contributing in no small measure to our disconnection from our

True Self. We will look at both from an entirely new perspective that allows us to give them the attention needed to receive the energetic messages they bring.

With a (w)holistic frame of reference and the component parts established, the next section will offer simple effective tools for accessing and interacting with the Heart Field. Key among them, Heart Centered Meditation is presented as a simple and essential tool for intentionally expanding our conscious awareness beyond just mind to the larger domain of the heart where the intersection of the physical, mental, and spiritual occurs and provides the natural experience of ourselves as whole beings.

Synchronizing our basic internal functions of breath, brainwaves and heartbeat results in what is called *coherence.* We experience this emotionally as inner peace. It is from this place of balance that we can be in coherence or harmony with not only ourselves, but also others, our environment, and the divine. *The Heart Field Effect*© research then documents our actual energy connections with others and demonstrates the effect our Heart Field has on those within range of our personal space and even those at any distance to which we direct our thoughts and the power of our heart.

Going beyond just our individual experience, we become aware of our connections not only with other people, but also all of life at both smaller and larger dimensions. As our frame of reference increases, our identity itself changes from a separate individual being to an integral part of a living matrix. From this vantage point the meaning and value of our choices and actions take on a new and larger significance. We see that what we feel, think, and do affects not only ourselves, but radiates within the energy environment, and alters the archetypes of the collective consciousness. The central role of consciousness and our essence as spirit fill the hole in the purely materialistic and humanistic worldviews. We will explore how the mental function is primarily masculine and electrical, the emotional, feeling heart function powerfully magnetic and feminine. This is not an issue of gender. Both genders have both principles operative within, although they develop differently. They are designed to work harmoniously together. The current overabundance of mental activity unbalanced by the feeling heart is a significant factor in the many imbalances we see in our world and experience within. As we grow in our appreciation and understanding of the 'invisible real' and the larger context of life beyond our individual being and even Earth centric focus, we expand our potential experience of life in ways unimaginable within the more limited perspective that makes up the current norm.

Gradually over the past four decades alternative views of everything from the nature of matter, the size of the universe, our understanding of mind, and the ability to access multiple resources through the internet have been emerging. With the advent of cyber communication we can directly connect with both others and information instantaneously; never before possible to the human community. While rightly celebrated for the many positive things this has made possible for us, less appreciated is the level of information overload and confusion resulting from reams of data without a corresponding level of reference to context, connection, relationship, and value.

Not many have the opportunity or desire to spend years of study learning the intricacies of biology, psychology, and religion. Fewer yet have had the opportunity to work professionally within each realm for significant lengths of time at locations all over the US. Yet with the benefit of that multiplicity one can see patterns emerge in a way not possible from a more singular perspective. With cross disciplinary training and experience, the impact of related aspects of each become more apparent to the function of the whole. With immense gratitude for having been privileged to have such a broad education and variety of experiences both professional and personal, it is my intention that this book provides a blueprint for connecting diverse fields of information, the essential keys to each, and practical tools to integrate them into daily living in ways that change your perceptions, enlarge your identity, and enhance both your awareness and experience of your personal power, and the experience of joy and fulfillment in your life.

I hope that as you read this book your heart will begin to sing its unique song and your spirit soar in delight of the life that is possible for you and for which you were intentionally created by the Source of all that is. May it be so.

2 WHAT IS THE HEART FIELD?

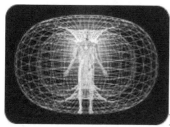

Figure 1. The Heart Field

It's all of who you are.

At its simplest your Heart Field is the Grand Organizing Design of who you are. As vibrating energy at our most foundational essence, the Heart Field describes both our structure and function at every level. It is exactly the same pattern found in all of nature, from the smallest atom to the largest universe. Duplicated in the geometric beauty of fractal unfolding, its underlying language is number and its expression the sacred geometry of connections and angles which determine its relationships. The main feature of a field is the force it exerts on the environment around it and what it attracts or allows to enter within. Like all force fields it is invisible to the naked eye, but can be recognized by its omnipresent effects on everything in its range.

The shape of the Heart Field, like all fields that we know of, is a torus. A three dimensional model of a torus is shaped like a donut. When we reduce our view to two dimensions it looks exactly like the pattern taken on by iron filings on a vibrating plate when exposed to frequency waves of music or sound that we've all seen in science museums. Another way of visualizing a torus is to imagine a sphere with a dimple at the top and bottom. The dimples indicate another key feature of a torus, which is that it is an open system. The dimple at the top and bottom show very clearly that energy can both enter into the torus and also exit from within. As we'll go into in greater detail in the next Chapter, this is a key characteristic of every torus.

Like all force fields the energy itself is invisible. Unlike earlier views of science where energy was thought to just randomly fly about in space until it bumps into something, we now observe that its movement follows definite patterns. What the torus describes is the pattern of energy movement, or toroidal flow. Were we to turn the torus ninety degrees and look at it again as a two dimensional drawing it would look like the familiar circle divided into sections of many familiar human charts and ritual patterns, for example horoscopes, medicine wheels, I-Ching, rose windows, etc. I'm sure you might think of more. Once we see the pattern we can recognize it everywhere. Looking at a single point of it moving through time we see a wave form. In Chapter Three we will take a detailed look at how it works.

At the turn of the century in 2002, journalist Lynn McTaggart wrote a best seller called <u>The Field: The Quest for the Secret Force of the Universe</u>. In it she compiled multi-disciplinary scientific evidence demonstrating the impact of mind, consciousness, and spirit on matter which provided compelling evidence of the reality of a pervasive life force energy. She noted, "For a number of decades respected scientists in a variety of disciplines all over the world have been carrying out well designed experiments whose results fly in the face of current biology and physics. Together these studies offer us copious information about the central organizing force governing our bodies and the rest of the cosmos. …at our most elemental, we are not a chemical reaction, but an energetic charge. Human beings and all living things are a coalescence of energy in *a field of energy connected to every other thing in the world* [italics mine]. This pulsating energy field is the central engine of our being and consciousness is our alpha and omega."

I was intrigued by the confirmation of what I had observed

clinically over many years in health care as both an RN and a psychotherapist. It is important to include the domain of the spiritual and the impact of consciousness and perception on a person's state of health. This work and others were the impetus in my return to academic studies once again to do my own personal exploration of how the body, mind, spirit dimensions of human being actually work. I wanted to know how we as health care professionals might work more effectively to provide, not isolated care of one aspect, but considering the particular in relation to the whole person. It was very clear that approaching the physical, mental, and spiritual individually in isolation from each other did not lead to good outcomes for patients. In the larger area of wellness, encompassing much more than just absence of disease, the necessity of integrating all of who we are into one cohesive whole eventually became the basis of a comprehensive whole systems approach of Heart Centered Wellness ™. We will examine the spiritual, emotional, mental, and physical components of this comprehensive approach in great detail in Part II, as well as describing simple specific practices in each area that contribute in particular ways to the well-being of the whole person. Wellness is a spiritual state and a DIY project!

In 2010, Claude Swanson, a well-known and highly regarded physicist published a voluminous and detailed tome, Life Force, The Scientific Basis. Now a classic in the field of energy medicine, this intricate work translated and collated the work of Russian researchers, especially Kozyrev, on the nature of life energy and the physics of how it works that is significantly different than our Western medical biochemical view. Unpacking scientific concepts of spin, torsion, and the underlying vibrational essence of all levels of life, Dr. Swanson made available to the Western scientific mind an entirely new way of thinking about our biological functioning largely unknown here and still ignored within the conventional world of US medical practice. For the average person the scientific detail and formulas, although brilliant, were beyond their comprehension as relatable to their experience of life in a meaningful way. Within the esoteric and exoteric literature there are vast quantities of information that go by the wayside of consideration by all but scholars due to the lack of our sense of contextual relevance. It is the purpose of this book to provide an overarching framework for these essential truths to be presented in such a way that their importance is clear and practical methods of application to daily life are provided.

In between these two paradigm shifting works relating to the energy basis of human function, I conducted and published research on *The Heart Field Effect©* as part of my doctoral work at Holos University. It documented the energetic connection (or what is called bio resonant entrainment in the language of science), of energy fields between persons that resulted in the synchronization of their heartbeats and altered both their physiology and their mental and emotional states. Implicit in this study was the presence of an energy field specific to the person. It is dynamic in nature, and encompasses all the aspects of their being previously only partially addressed within the various traditions of knowledge related to human being. In the West we refer to body, mind, and spirit. In Eastern systems terms like chi, qi, aura, meridians, nadis, and chakras are used to describe the nature, structure, and pathways of life energy. Although science had established decades ago that our earlier concepts of matter and energy were erroneous and that everything is energy in its different forms and expressions, our Western medical science continues to operate out of the old paradigm that regards what is physical as real, and all else either illusory or not relevant. This study and others were the early scientific confirmation of what has been observed by traditional practitioners of many spiritual disciplines all over the world for centuries, but is still largely discounted by our current medical system which relies almost exclusively on biochemical data and its alteration with pharmaceuticals to treat both physical and mental/emotional disease symptoms. The presence of a specific dynamic force field that encompasses all of who we are, and which interacts vibrationally with both our inner and outer environments to affect and effect life functions in accordance to universal principles is the Heart Field. Recognizing the presence of this energy force field provides us with a larger conceptual picture of who we are, at the same time placing us firmly within the context of integral parts of even larger wholes. It unifies both Eastern and Western viewpoints by recognizing their contributions but placing them, not as opposing viewpoints, but as two halves of the same whole. Validating the primacy of energy and vibration as the foundational level from whence all else originates, this larger context also shifts our understanding of the control center of our human life from its long standing location in the brain and its electrical impulses, to the heart and the vibrational communication of its beat constantly aligning the many functions of the body into a synchronized, unified whole. In Chapter three we will look at how this works.

In the big picture, the beating of our hearts creates an electromagnetic field that extends well beyond our physical body. Invisible to most, its impact on every aspect of our lives is profound. Although its reality is documented and measureable with simple instruments, its existence unknown to most, it defines who we are. This is your Heart Field.

The Heart Field is the energy reality of all of who you are. Understanding what it is and how it works provides us with the ability to interact with it consciously with intention. Without that awareness and skills to direct it, we are not much more than reactive beings. Let's take a look at some of its components.

If you mention chakras or meridians, most people will have at least heard the terms, and some can give fairly detailed definitions or descriptions of what they are. But say 'Heart Field' and you are liable to draw a blank stare. Everyone knows that we all have a heart—that little fist sized muscle hidden safely in the center of our chest that pumps our blood around. Years ago when I was studying to become a nurse, the heart got one part of a Chapter in the anatomy and physiology textbook. It was described as the center point of the body's circulatory system whose sole function was to contract regularly, thereby pumping the body's approximately 5 quarts of blood through its thousands of miles of blood vessels, taking the oxygen obtained as it went through the lungs and delivering it to each cell of the body. There an exchange would take place. The cell would be given the oxygen necessary for the cell to do its work, and return its waste products to the blood to be carried to the kidneys, liver, and lungs for excretion. This was the heart's total function. A bit more was then said about its structure and how it did its work. It was acknowledged that the cells that make up the heart are different than any other cells in the body. They could not be described as either 'striated' or 'smooth' like all the other muscle cells everywhere else in the body. Rather, heart cells were described as having a 'figure 8' structure not found anywhere else in the body. Picture a mini infinity symbol— divine humor at its finest. It was noted that these cells included a special property; each one able to contract on its own. Overall the heart had an electrical system that makes up its communication system and conveys an impulse down a branch of special nerve fibers so all the cells can contract together at the same time, creating a contraction of the whole heart at the same time, and in a simple mechanical action pushing all the blood within out into the blood vessels and around the whole body.

Many, perhaps most, still think of this as the heart's only purpose. It's ironic that this most basic function has been accepted for years by intelligent highly trained physicians as largely true, ignoring even basic physics of what size heart would be needed to pump our blood in the manner described through the many miles of blood vessels it has to go through on its trip through the body. Even an undergraduate engineering student given the actual volume of blood and distance traveled as a homework assignment can determine that the heart would need to be many times bigger than it is to perform its function in this manner.

Today, medical science now recognizes that the heart has its own nervous system, and even has been able to determine that the electrical signals communicating between the brain and heart— long assumed to be the brain directing the heart—in fact originate first in the heart, then go to the brain rather than the other way around. There is a whole new medical subspecialty of neurocardiology which studies how this works. The implications of it remain unexamined and the term 'Heart Field' is still largely unknown. If it is acknowledged at all, it is described as the bubble shaped perimeter extending for several feet around the body in which one is able to pick up the signal of the heartbeat. It is mentioned, then ignored, as if it has no significance whatsoever. Like the old story of the Native Americans unable to see the approaching ship on the horizon of the sea until it was pointed out by their medicine man, because they had never seen one, because it doesn't fit into the current medical paradigm the Heart Field, although self-evident, it isn't seen. Even within the holistic community of energy practitioners its significance has not yet been fully appreciated. The most conscientious among us still fall prey to trying to fit new information into old conceptual frameworks, thereby losing the immensity of the shift implicated in our new understanding.

The reality of the Heart Field is so much more! Our heartbeat which begins a mere 4 or 5 weeks after conception, long before there's any need to pump blood, is the drumbeat of our life. Our own unique vibrational signature, within the resonant vibrations of its beating lies both the information and the coordinating capacity to not only circulate our blood, but in fact to serve as the primary communication system of our whole being. This includes not only the physical, but as we move forward we will discover how the heartbeat conveys through its frequency signals all the information needed to monitor and regulate our internal physiological function. It connects our physical function with our mental perceptions, monitoring and responding to our emotional state, and also conveys information externally, outward into the environment broadcasting our state of the moment energy reality into the world around us.

Several of the world's oldest medical whole person systems in practice for several thousand years in contrast to our Western model which is only around two hundred years old, have incorporated aspects of the Heart Field in their models. For instance, the chakras and meridians known in other medical systems like Ayurveda and Traditional Chinese Medicine are parts of the Heart Field. In *The Heart Field* we connect the understanding of the individual aspects into a comprehensive, coherent, unified whole. Much more about this in Chapters three and four.

Switching gears entirely, the other major domain of authority in our world, religion, has consistently recognized the power of the heart as the spiritual center of our being. The heart as a source of power and connection to others and the divine has historically been nearly universally acknowledged. While there are a variety of ways of saying it, all spiritual wisdom refers to the heart as 'the seat of the soul,' 'the still small voice within,' the location of our true self—usually in contrast to the term false self, defined as the separate ego. This is the philosophical recognition of the Heart Field as the domain of human life in which we experience ourselves as connected to others and to the divine or all that is.

Love, which I define as experienced connection and the substance of all that is, is always expressed consciously or unconsciously as originating in the heart. Many of our automatic responses demonstrate this. When we greet someone we feel close to, we open our arms and put our heart against theirs, physically uniting our Heart Fields in a quite literal way. In the esoteric world the hands are understood to be extensions of the heart, conveying its vibrational reality through touch. The power of touch has long been acknowledged as a basic human need. Now our scientific understanding is providing an energetic explanation of what occurs at multiple levels when we touch. When someone is distressed we instinctively hug them, putting our heart next to theirs and often patting them on the back, a practice of tapping we'll look at more closely later on that removes energy interferences much like shaking dirt out of a rug or brushing lint or dandruff off a shirt or coat. A mother automatically rocks a distressed baby to soothe it. All of these are ways we will see of restoring balance and grounding to the energy flow of our Heart Field that we already know and use without even realizing it.

The Heart Field, encompassing all of our being, has multiple dimensions. There are three that we need to be aware of. We are all aware of our physical heart. It is a single muscle composed of a unique type of muscle cell found nowhere else within the body. We can hear and feel its constant beat reassuringly present every moment of our lives. Most also know that heart disease; literally heart dis-ease energetically, is the number one cause of death in the Western cultures. This sobering fact reflects an unavoidable report card of our life style choices upon our energy function. Reason enough to compel us to examine in greater depth its role beyond the obvious blood pumping function as the crucial structure of our circulatory system. In Five we will address specific practices to keep our physical heart healthy that come from the perspective of our physical heart as an energetic as well as physical structure.

Because we often talk about our heart as the center of our emotions, we are somewhat aware of the emotional heart—we'll unpack this in much greater detail in Chapter Seven. For the moment it suffices to realize that we have vastly misunderstood what feelings and emotions are. Because of this lack of understanding we have largely mishandled them; opting often to attempt to control or manage them rather than paying attention to them for the vital energy messengers they really are. In reality they are our perception of energy movement; e—motion, within and between the dimensions of our own being internally; and likewise of our field interactions with others, the collective unconscious, and other life externally. We ignore, dismiss, or sublimate them to our distress and peril. Misunderstanding emotions is one of the biggest obstacles to our self-knowledge, our relationships, and our continued growth as human beings. Our emotional heart is the dynamic GPS of our lives.

Third is our experience of our soul or spirit. The terms are used somewhat differently in different traditions but our purpose here is not to debate different religious philosophies, but rather to recognize the spiritual dimension of the Heart Field as the inner experiential location of unity with all of life, and ultimately our own divine nature. Often described as union with God and all of life, this expansive domain also provides us with our most exquisite experience of our essential self, or what has been called True Self. This Self experiences being as an integral part of both much larger and much smaller experiences of life itself. Inextricably interconnected with all that is, there is no sense of separation here, although individuality remains and rather than diminished is heightened. In the transcendent spiritual teachings that have composed most of world religion for the past several thousands of years, the focus was on union with God as an external, out of body experience of consciousness. This mental experience perhaps most clearly delineated in Buddhism, focuses on training mind and considers physical or material reality as illusory. While in one sense true—there is no 'matter', all is energy—in practice it has been distorted to devalue the physical dimension as unreal and locates us as an observer rather than participant in the experiences and processes of daily life. The mental layer of our Heart Field will be explored in Chapter Six.

Lincoln's injunction that "A house divided against itself cannot stand," is not limited to external reality. Our focus on what is only one half of spiritual reality has not only divided us over which half is real, but also blinded us to the cyclical nature of life in this dimension as well as all others. The focus on transcendence alone causes us to miss the other half of spiritual reality—immanence. This was the central teaching of Christ. "I and the Father are one, and I am in Him and He is in me." He went on to add that we are all part of the same One body; not by our beliefs as organized Christianity has falsely insisted, but as a statement of literal truth about our very nature. Divinity resides within us. Whether we recognize it or not does not alter the reality. Although patriarchal control of Christianity resulted in transcendent bias, the central role of the feminine heart remains within the religion whose focus is on Love. The ignorance of 'the universe within' or 'Holy Spirit' has distorted our perceptions of who we are and also our notions of who God is. By missing half of the message of Spirit, we ended up with adversarial religious views, further dividing our wholeness to the detriment of understanding that ONE includes both aspects of spirit; transcendence AND immanence. It is not surprising that the Christian church has fractured into hundreds of fragments, a stark contrast to Jesus' message of one body. Chapter Eight covers the spiritual aspects of our Heart Field.

For the last several thousand years, most major world religions have placed Spirit as something outside ourselves, leaving us with a residual inner sense of somehow being 'not enough.' This ubiquitous experience, looked at as pathology by psychology and unable to be fully treated by cognitive behavioral therapy alone, is actually an accurate experience of being conscious at only the level of mind and perception of oneself as individual. It feels like not enough because it is an incomplete experience of the whole of who we are. Only when we also embody our spirit along with our mind and body do we experience the whole of the human experience. To paraphrase de Chardin, we are most fully divine when we are grounded in being fully human. Only by expanding our consciousness to the level of our hearts can we experience ourselves as enough; an integrated whole being of body, mind, and spirit.

From this perspective we can see that the sense of not enough is actually the loving beckoning of the Divine, encouraging us to grow into an awareness of all of who we are. It cannot be healed at the mental level by changing our thinking, or at the physical level by altering our biochemistry with drugs. Although sometimes temporarily helpful, by not addressing cause, both fail to provide the lasting transformation that is only possible within the larger consciousness of our spiritual hearts. Learning how to expand our conscious awareness to all levels of our heart is not difficult, although requiring regular practice to incorporate into our lives in a way that alters our perceptions and responses, our self-confidence and actions. Practices that develop this heart level of consciousness are detailed in Chapters Seven, Eight, and Ten.

Both science and spiritual conventions have left out consciousness as an inherent factor in all that we observe, choose, and create. Partly this is due to lack of any agreed upon definition of what consciousness is. It was less than two hundred years ago that Freud coined the term and identified three levels to consciousness: the id, ego, and super-ego. To this, his student and close colleague Carl Jung added the Collective Unconscious, a place of archetypal patterns that had an influence on us that we are totally unaware of, but which have huge impact at the unconscious or subconscious levels. Both were professionally ostracized at the time, but their contributions to our human understanding have evolved into the discipline of psychology. Now an integral part of our health care system, the impact of mental and emotional factors on our physical health is much more appreciated, though socially still suspect to some and the recipient of negative regard by many. To our detriment, the exclusion of this capacity of awareness or attention as a key feature of our human function and potential has largely limited our science to the single dimension of the physical removed from its context within the whole. Our spiritual realization seen as subjective inner state disconnected from the outer world around us.

The Heart Field is the holographic energy vehicle encompassing all of these dimensions of our human being. It provides us with a way of knowing who we are at the deepest level of experienced reality. Understanding it at even a very basic level provides the conceptual framework that integrates all of the parts into a unified whole. It allows us to make sense of what seemed before to be disparate, unconnected parts of ourselves. It is congruent with all that we know of both larger and smaller whole systems. Beyond understanding our own personal function better, it re-locates human being back within the Living Matrix of all of life at every level. It shifts our perception of who we are from an outside observer to an integral aspect of the larger whole, whose thoughts, feelings, and behavior have impact not just on ourselves, but also on the environment around us.

As the implications of this higher understanding of who we are filter into our moment to moment awareness, our identity is changed. No longer thinking of ourselves as separate individuals whose perceptions, thoughts, choices, and actions don't affect anyone but us--and therefore are no one else's concern--we grow to understand our interconnections and become responsible out of an entirely different realization that we truly are all in this together.

While the dangers of living in the either/or world of duality and its victim mentality become ever more evident in the increasing insanity that surrounds us, it is clear that the voice of reason alone is not enough to save us from ourselves. A larger more inclusive worldview is essential. The truth of the old saying, mind makes a wonderful servant, but a terrible master, confronts us in all the destructive human interactions we see around us with increasing frequency. The masculine electric principle of brain and its separate sense of self as ego dominate unbalanced by the magnetic feminine principle and intuition of the heart. Our two brain hemispheres while wonderful at pattern recognition and the analysis of the intellect, are inadequate in many ways for being the control center of our life. As my friend and colleague Dr Dan Benor says, it's like mistaking the TV set for the source of the programming. While the electric impulses of the brain as life control central is still the prevalent scientific mindset, there is mounting evidence that this role rightly belongs to the Heart Field.

The vibrational information carried with each heartbeat is distributed instantaneously throughout the water of our bodies and surrounding environment much faster than an electrical impulse from the brain can transmit via neurons. It not only communicates, regulates, and synchronizes our internal needs and function, our heart has also been documented to pulse photons of light with each beat radiating information to the external environment around us as torsion. Torsion also appears to be able to be directed with mental intention instantaneously outside the space/time continuum, powered by the intensity and focused ability of our heart's development. Prayer has long been known to work non-locally in healing and other ways. Much remains to be learned, but the Heart

Field seems to incorporate the anomalies unexplainable in our current medical model while including the functions we understand biochemically from a perhaps more foundational level.

The experience of Myrtle and Charles Fillmore which developed into the Unity Movement are illustrative. As lifelong Christians, when Myrtle was confronted with advanced tuberculosis she prayed daily, believing Jesus' teachings to be literally true. She persisted with full confidence and over time she was healed. Likewise her husband Charles who had been born with one leg shorter than the other causing a limp, also began practicing what has become known as affirmative prayer. This prayer takes as a given that at the level of our spirit we are always complete, whole, and healthy. They affirmed this highest level of truth as present now, not only with the focus of thought, but with the power of heart to vibrationally modulate life frequencies. This replaced the distorted energy pattern in their field to which their physical bodies then conformed. His leg lengthened. Soon friends who knew of their story began asking how they did it and began applying it to their own concerns. The stories of healings spread, and in a time when Jesus' teachings were either seen as miracles or metaphor, Unity developed as the practical walk of Christianity. Based in Unity Village in Lees Summit, MO, Silent Unity to this day offers affirmative prayer twenty-four hours a day, seven days a week for anyone calling with a request.

This is just one example of many that could be cited, understood in many different ways by people of faith. Unexplainable by medical science, most just accept the healing results as an article of faith, not feeling the need for knowing just how it happened. Yet our perceptions and our ability to be conscious of dimensions of our own being that operate beyond the limited range of our five senses can be so much more than most of us experience now. We know this because there are, and always have been other human beings who do experience them. These folks do not possess different human capacities than all of us. They just for one reason or another have learned to be aware of them and to use them. The capacity is inherent within each of us.

As with any of our human capabilities the cliché, 'use it or lose it' applies. The potential remains, but atrophy diminishes what it can do. This is true of the muscles and bones of our physical self and equally true of our minds and mental function. As one of the principles of how life works, why would it be any different in the realm of emotion and spirit? Yet it is also true that we make no attempt to choose something, or use some aspect of ourselves that we don't know exists, or that we have not been taught how to use. We have historically placed those persons who do demonstrate these higher aspects of human capability on pedestals, worshipping them as super humans while missing the message they bring, thinking it can't possibly apply to us mere mortals. It's time for us to revisit their teachings and examples. If we do so with an open mind we will discover that none of them was looking for self-aggrandizement or ego inflation. In the face of human glorification they uniformly remained humble and often provided extreme demonstrations of what is possible, while calling each of us to recognize and grow into these same qualities within ourselves. All clearly stressed that there is only One, and we are all particular manifestations of the One divine Source of all that is.

While it is true that we each are better at and more inclined to some things than others, our differentiation likely serves the same purpose as the cells of our body. While all beginning from the same two cells, as they grow and multiply some grow into bone cells, some heart cells, some liver cell, some blood or brain cells. We do not label some as better, or more gifted than others. We recognize that they each have a particular purpose that contributes something essential to the whole. And so while it is true that there are significant differences among us, all are needed to function together as a unified whole for optimal function of the whole humanity being that we are. Likewise, each religious tradition developed in a particular place and culture, its teachings relevant to the setting. Differing words, names, rituals and traditions do not diminish the reality of the One Source. Only the egoic self perceives these as separate, and therefore competing religions where for one to be right, others must be wrong. Like individual human development, humanity as a whole has had developmental stages. Our earliest times were spent on physical survival and development. For the last several thousands of years we have primarily developed mentally, and for most their consciousness was focused in this realm with minimal awareness of the others. It is a new age, and it is not an accident of nature that each of us is present at the shift as humanity makes yet another leap up the ladder of evolution.

If you have read this far, you have already noted that this is a different kind of book. It is not a science book, although references to scientific studies that demonstrate some aspect of the reality of The Heart Field will be noted throughout and referenced at the end for those readers who would like more details about specific aspects mentioned. It is not a religious book, favoring some particular religious perspective over others, but it is spiritual and will not avoid using spiritual terminology. As you will see further on I define Wellness as a spiritual state. It is not a psychology book, though the mental and emotional are also examined from a perspective of their roles in the function of the whole human being. It is not another formulaic recipe of the three (or four, or five, or seven) easy steps to becoming rich, beautiful, and successful.

Most of the information within is found in other places, sometimes many other places. So why write yet another book? It is my opinion that while we are almost drowning in a constantly growing tsunami of information, what is too often missing is a map that helps us to connect the dots of the many pieces of our lives in a way that offers a whole context. The Heart Field provides an energetic explanation for the dimensions of our being, how they are connected and interact, and how to consciously access each or all of them at will and with intention. This book presents the essential energy principles of the levels of our being and offers an explanation of how we can become more response-able owners. Connections and relationships not visible when looking at each in isolation will be readily apparent as we view them as an amazing and integrated whole. Specific tools and practices within each level offer simple and practical ways to do this. You are so much more than you yet realize. This book is for those who want to embark on the adventure.

The Heart Field as yet is largely unknown to most, but as vibrational medicine becomes the reality of twenty first century healthcare as the famous cardiac surgeon Dr Oz proclaimed recently on TV, its presence and power are beginning to emerge within mainstream consciousness. The urgent need for the return of the feminine principle and power of the heart found in all of us, male and female alike, is again needed to provide the full context of life in balance. The dimensions of our being intersect within our heart, and becoming conscious at the heart level is the necessary means to experiencing our unity both within ourselves and as a unified humanity. A unified humanity with a conscious Heart Field becomes the Noosphere or mind of Earth herself, and together we ascend to the next level of life being.

3 HOW DOES IT WORK ?

It's one thing for science to state that there is no longer matter and energy, there is only energy, but what does it mean that we are energy? If the Heart Field is the energy that composes all of who we are; our physical structure, our mental function, our emotions, and our spirit, how does it work as a coordinated whole? To see ourselves in this way requires a virtual paradigm shift in how we see ourselves and in our perspective of human anatomy and physiology. It offers us a simple and elegant explanation for understanding ourselves in a much more unified way. Energy is always about purposeful action. It carries many bits of information. They have always been there and are increasingly coming into our conscious awareness. Contrary to the tendency of current complexity thinking, which separates things into ever smaller bits, the Heart Field is profoundly simple in its unifying completeness. A field is an area of force having an effect upon all that is within it, without altering its nature in the process.

Many fine explanations of our subtle energy anatomy have become available to us in the West over the past several decades. With the growing popularity of meditation, yoga and the internal martial arts like T'ai Chi Chuan, and the energy balancing of Qi Gong, we have been able to see and feel the effects of energy. As we become able to feel it, these systems have also taught us how to begin to direct our life energies mentally. In the last quarter of the twentieth century Reiki started being taught, instilling a spiritual dimension to energy work. Healing Touch, Therapeutic Touch, Barbara Brennen and Donna Eden began dispersing the knowledge of how to provide healing with simple manipulation of the body's energy field. Energy practitioners began to abound, with little knowledge or oversight of their actual skills or proficiency. Public response varied from considering them miracle workers to charlatans. With these new to us practices has come a curiosity about what life energy is and how it works.

While the descriptions of subtle energy fields (the aura and its layers), pathways it travels within the body (the hara, meridians and nadis), and awareness that our physical bodies are surrounded by multiple layers of energy corresponding to the different dimensions of our human being have been eye opening, they have frequently come couched in terminology of other cultures and ancient times when they were known. Without a common frame of reference we fail to see its applicability to our lives. For energy practitioners and those readers who want much more detail there are several excellent and highly detailed descriptions of our energy anatomy. I highly recommend Desda Zuckerman's <u>Your Sacred Anatomy: An Owner's Guide to the Human Energy Structure</u>. It's over four hundred pages are packed with beautiful illustrations and minutely detailed description of each aspect of our human energy system. For the average person wanting to understand ourselves as energy rather than biochemistry in our daily experience, we need an accurate but simple explanation.

The recognition of the Heart Field provides us with a context into which all the partial bits of what we have come to realize energetically can be seen and understood as aspects of one whole system—the human—and how we are integrated within a living matrix of both larger and smaller other systems. It is not a new discovery, but congruent with our time and frames of reference. It provides a context to understand the parts better than we are able to in isolation, and also to put them into practice in our lives more easily. New information is more readily retained and clearer to us when we have a context for it.

In earlier times when the human worldview was aligned with nature and its cycles, human beings knew themselves as inherent parts of nature and all life. In what most of us were taught was a primitive worldview everything, including human beings, was regarded as part of a larger whole. In the few remaining indigenous cultures this is still the prevailing construct. For those of us in the 'civilized' world and especially in Western cultures, an entirely different worldview came into being over time. First we separated science and spirit, making them discrete and operating by different rules. With the professionalization of science, man observed, explored, and described what he could perceive with his five senses. Only that which is measureable and predictable was considered valid. Everything invisible was considered irrelevant and left entirely out of consideration as having any effect on material reality. It was not real. It was superstition, irrelevant, and irrational. The agreed upon separation of science and religion entrenched this perspective and created separation in who we understood ourselves to be.

Concepts of subjectivity and objectivity came into being and separated the inner and outer worlds. If it was spiritual in nature, it was regarded as the purview of religion, an agreed upon 'no man's land' for science where beliefs were considered obstacles clouding ability to observe an objective and real reality understood to exist outside of us. This became the prevailing perspective and continued as the main cultural perspective throughout the twentieth century. It is still the most common frame of reference for many. Yet as our lives became increasingly fragmented and unsatisfying in some deep sense, we began to look for something that would make sense of it all.

As technology came into being it became increasingly dominant in validating everything from the state of our internal processes to documenting the tiniest of subatomic particles and the largest of planets and galaxies millions of light years away. It was rightly celebrated for extending our ability to validate realities beyond the narrow limitations of our five senses. Somehow, rather than reminding us of the vast dimensions beyond our sensory limitations, within the world of science the materialistic mindset continued the practice of regarding as unreal anything that we cannot measure and predict. Technology itself became regarded as a sign of our superiority, rather than a poor imitation of human capabilities we have not yet become aware of or developed. Like everything, technology itself is neutral. We have many examples of how it can be used constructively or destructively. My point is not to denigrate technology, but to remind us not to create yet another dependence upon external objects the substitution of which keeps us from recognizing, honing, and using our own inherent abilities and power. Our present perspective and understanding of ourselves has come out of this materialistic reductionism of conventional science. It pervades every area of human endeavor. New information alone is not enough. We have learned that we are energy. But we also need a new way of seeing.

Holistic perspective in many ways is the opposite of material reductionism. Reducing everything to the smallest part possible and then studying and describing it in isolation as a separate thing misses critical aspects of seeing the whole. Connections, relationships and interactions are all lost when a part is taken out of context. Likewise limiting our examination to only 2D or 3D is insufficient for perceiving the holographic reality we understand energy to be. For instance, electrons do not flicker in and out of existence. This contradicts the very first premise of energy, that it is neither created nor destroyed; it just changes forms. To that we can now add, and sometimes dimensions. So what appears to be appearing and disappearing are actually the electrons going back and forth from one dimension to another. Because we haven't yet been able to record that on some instrument it remains unseen even though it flies in the face of the first law of physics.

To understand who we are as beings of light and energy, more is required than merely assimilating new pieces of information into the contemporary mental context. As we look at how the Heart Field works we will need to expand the range of our viewing. Whole new realms not previously recognized as relevant become important. It's a larger frame of reference based in actual experience rather than conceptual. We must also shift our perspective from one of taking apart and separating to one of integration of all aspects seeing them in connection to the whole. Connections and relationships are key, and they are crucial elements missing in materialism. Understanding the Heart Field provides both a comprehensive energy description that integrates the energy elements we have begun to be aware of, and points us toward means of accessing them experientially.

The first thing to note is that we are energy beings of light. Once we get away from the old notion that we are matter; something concrete, separate, and of a different composition than energy, we need a different definition of our physical nature. We know that what we refer to as dark matter and energy is still 99+% space. We have a holographic structure very similar to that seen in science fiction movies, for instance on the Holodeck in Star Trek. In these venues a projector organizes light into three dimensional figures and setting with which the actors are then able to interact as if in real life. As we continue to learn more about how our own DNA emits photons, patterning every aspect of our existence, it may well be that science fiction is more closely aligned with our actual states of being than we have recognized.

The most basic qualities of energy are dynamism or movement, and power. Merriam-Webster Dictionary offers a number of definitions for energy, several of which are relevant to us: 1. A dynamic quality or the capacity of acting or being active. 2. A usually positive spiritual force; the energy flowing through all people. 3. Vigorous exertion of power or what we call effort. 4. Usable power. All of these relate to the Heart Field to some extent. One thing not listed, and not yet agreed upon by all scientists is energy as a carrier of information. This brings us to what information is, another quagmire in the scientific landscape. Bring your shovel and let's get to the basics that concern us.

For our purposes it is only necessary to know that we are energy beings of light, and that our life energy moves in a toroidal pattern of flow identical to that of planets, atoms, or any forms of life that we know. Two characteristics of tori bear mention. One is that a torus is an open system, allowing outside energy to enter, and also emitting energy in the form of biophotons and creation of torsion. The flow pattern includes vortices between the various layers and with the outside environment as vehicles of transmission for energy and information from one layer or dimension to another, and for using life energy for specific functions. This transport system is the role of our chakras. Although changing post 2012 shift with new energies on Earth that were not available to us before, the classical understanding was that each human being has seven chakras. The crown chakra at the top of our head, and the root chakra at the base of our spine comprised the vertical dimension. The function of the crown chakra was to connect us with our higher or spiritual self, while the root chakra grounded us to Mother Earth. Chakras two through six made up the horizontal connections, each having both a back and front vortex. The back portion related to will and the front to emotion. Each one has a particular area of energy control within the body and correlates to a specific gland and organ system. The language of energy is feelings, and so we experience energy movement within our field as both physical sensation and mental emotion.

Equally important, as we touched on in the previous Chapter, consciousness itself impacts every aspect of our being. Although we are at the 'tip of the iceberg' stage in our understanding of what it is and how it impacts us, its central role in all human function is inescapable. Likewise our sense of time has been impacted by calendars and mechanical clocks that aren't in alignment with Natural Time and need adjustment. It affects our perceptual synchronization with our own internal rhythms and also alignment with others, nature, and Earth herself. These are key factors that impact our energy alignment internally and externally and will be discussed in Chapters on accessing your Heart Field.

As the owner and operator of the particular human being that we are, we may not be interested in every little detail, but as anyone who has tried to skip the instructions and operate a new gadget can attest, it's usually a good idea to have some idea of what it is, how it fits together and how to make it work in the way it is designed to, if we want it to function efficiently and do its job well. While the Heart Field is quite complete and functional on its own, as we grow more familiar with the emotional and spiritual dimensions and its vibrational communication through beat to beat harmonics of frequency modulation, our appreciation grows exponentially. As we develop our ability to be conscious within our heart as well as our head, a skill learned through the inner awareness of heart meditation, our ability to direct the immense power of our heart in specific ways grows more and more. In the last Chapter we defined what we know so far about what the Heart Field is. In this Chapter we want to get an overview of how it works.

At its most basic, the Heart Field is our power, communication and alignment source for body, mind, and spirit. This is true at every level of our being; body, mind, and spirit. Each cell of our physical heart emits photons with every beat. Quite a bit of research is underway in multiple locations exploring to what extent focused intention may direct these photons in particular ways. Perhaps one day soon we may understand the workings of prayer. Previously only the physical heart and its circulatory function were recognized in human health. The mechanical movement of expansion and contraction were observed to pump blood throughout our body. As a transportation system only two things required attention: rhythm and volume. Conventional medicine has mapped well the electrical conduction system that contracts the heart muscle, and documented in detailed fashion the normal sinus rhythm of a healthy heartbeat, and the various dysrhythmias or irregular heartbeats that can cause malfunction or even death. They have also developed electrical, technological, and chemical means for effecting alteration when necessary. Beyond rhythm and volume, the biochemistry involved is medicine's chief way of influencing the physical heart. Therapeutic efforts are limited to three modalities: mechanical restructuring through surgery, electrical rhythm adjustments such as defibrillation, cardioversion, and pacemakers, and biochemical or drug use to affect changes in blood volume and other circulatory interactions. No consideration is routinely given to mental and spiritual factors beyond a cursory nod to stress that is then largely ignored in treatment.

When we look at the whole Heart Field we see much more. Certainly the physical heart is central to our physical life. But that is just the beginning. Our spiritual traditions have always identified the heart as the 'seat of the soul' or where the voice of spirit speaks to us. Instinctively when describing our emotions we say things like, you touched my heart, or my heart is broken. These and many other common sayings we can recall, indicate our inner knowing of the heart as our emotional center. We build defending walls around our emotional heart according to the level of safety we require. These are a primary source of energy obstruction which can lead to emotional and physical disease if left unattended to. So when we speak of the heart we are already aware that it actually has at least three dimensions: physical, emotional, and spiritual. To understand what it is and how it works we need to look at all three. The neutral language of energy and physics offers a place to start. If details bore you, feel free to just skip this section. It is included for those who like more detail.

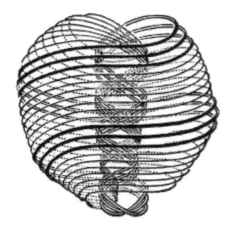

Figure 2. The Heart Field bidirectional flow.

Earlier in Fig.1, a much simpler and stylized picture of The Heart Field shows the torus configuration that is the hallmark of energy flow in every living system. It shows the energy flow pattern in a north/south polar view. As an open system, energy can enter or leave from the top or bottom. That would be the crown chakra and root chakra for those familiar with them.

In Fig. 2, a horizontal view of the Heart Field's toroidal flow allows us to see this bidirectional energy flow and its crossover intersections we know as chakras, except for the crown chakra which is actually 12-18" above our heads. There is yet a third energy channel, not shown in the drawing, called the hara and aligned with the spine which would appear going up through the middle space if included.

By bidirectional flow we mean that energy is simultaneously flowing upward in a toroidal flow pattern and downward in same toroidal pattern. Downward flow is centripetal, counterclockwise or what a physicist would call left spin. Upward flow is centrifugal, clockwise, or right spin. These vortex flows are radial or spiraling rather than straight up and down. You can see this clearly in Fig. 3, where the first diagram shows the inner flow and the second the outer field wall formed by their interaction.

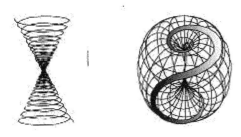

Figure 3. The double vortex

Nassim Haramein, a well-known physicist gave a description of a vortex in one of his TEDX talks as a tapered cavity whose spin produces a force (thrust) not attributable to classical electromagnetic phenomena, and therefore potentially demonstrating interaction with quantum vacuum virtual plasma. Or in non-physics terminology, that the spinning vortices that make up our chakras may interact with the part of the universe that we know of as dark energy. The smallest things we know of, photons or quanta, are light and align with masculine and electric qualities in nature. The dark energy makes up the field of infinite possibilities (nothing yet manifest) and aligns with feminine and magnetic qualities. We have known about and studied the properties of light for a very long time. It has only been a few years since we have realized that space is not empty as we had thought, but is made up of dark matter and energy and composes more than 99% of the universe. Much of the current state of our knowledge in this arena is speculative, but interesting to contemplate the potential for having an explanation for how it is we interact with the divine source; how prayer and intention work may find their answers here.

You'll notice that the toroidal flow pattern illustrated in Fig. 2 is shaped precisely like the muscle of our physical heart. When dissected the physical heart is revealed to be a single muscle, rectangular in shape. In keeping with the 'as above, so below' of perennial wisdom, if you were to take both ends of this rectangle and twist each end at the same time in opposite directions you would quickly see that the muscle folds itself into the four chambers of our heart. Its inherent beat then circulates not just our blood, but also the vibrational frequencies that keep all our life processes synchronized like a harmony of chords, conveying needed information to every cell of our body instantaneously. The iron that makes up much of our red blood cells maintains the magnetic properties of the Heart Field within the distribution throughout the body.

In a fetus just 4 or 5 weeks old a heartbeat is already present. Medicine has no explanation for how this happens, or how the small clump of identical cells then differentiate into the amazing miracle of a body we are born with nine months later. Within vibrational medicine it is given that information rides on energy, and it is the theory of this author that your heartbeat is your unique vibrational signature, spiritual in nature, and that this beat forms the magnetoelectric field which then initiates, directs, regulates and maintains first the development of your body, and then your mind, personality, and all the attributes that you think of as you, continuously throughout your life in physical form on Earth.

You may have noticed that I transposed the usual electromagnetic term into magnetoelectric. This is not a misprint. Our head and our heart are designed to work together. Both have electromagnetic fields created by their functional activity. While the brain's function is primarily electrical and action oriented in nature, corresponding to the masculine principle, the heart's primary function is magnetic, attracting, and corresponds to the feminine principle. Both males and females of course have both electric and magnetic properties. They do not refer to gender, and the principles always work together in synergistic fashion. In contrast to the brain however, the electric aspect of the heart's field is fifty times stronger than that of the brain, and its magnetic aspect is five thousand to six thousand times stronger, and encompasses the brain's field along with all of the other specific organ system fields of the body within the confines of our Heart Field. Hence the need to rethink exactly how it is our bodies work.

In the nested model popularized by Ken Wilber, each field out offers a higher function while encompassing everything within the smaller ones nested within it. From this perspective it becomes visibly obvious in looking at the Heart Field that it is our hearts, not our brains that connect and direct all our life processes in a coherent way. As soon as you see it, it becomes hard to understand how we didn't see it sooner. Recognizing this shifts everything we know about human function, and makes sense of quite a bit that didn't seem to fit in the brain centered model. It shifts our whole perspective in myriad ways.

Put in a more poetic way, the mystical artist Rassouli has said, "Both feminine and masculine powers are creative, but it is the feminine power that experiences the full circle of creating, nurturing, and transforming us as the participants in the creative process. That power...knows and recognizes the guiding light and surrenders to it. As people of the twenty first century, we need to allow the feminine voice and heart to guide us in making our transformation into becoming residents of a united world." To that I would add that we need to expand our conscious awareness to the heart level in order to be able to hear its voice of intuition. That skill is developed through the inner vision established with a practice of meditation. The mindfulness meditations have been very helpful in making persons aware of their thoughts, a necessary and important first step, but insufficient to change us at the most causal level of energy. The intellect is a limited faculty and aware of itself only as ego perceiving itself as separate, and operating as thought. As Einstein reminded us, we cannot solve a problem at the level at which it was created. Since a sense of separation is at the core of our feeling of 'not enough' it becomes apparent that healing is not possible at the mental level, and we must go beyond. We perceive energy as feeling. Heart meditation takes the meditation process to the next level and helps us become aware of our feelings, the energetic and symbolic language of our hearts.

As we learn more about our energy nature and the vibration and resonance process of communication and connection we can begin to interact with those energies with attention and intention. The spiritual corollary is free will. While it is an inherent potential within all human beings, what psychology has shown us repeatedly is that minus conscious awareness, our choices are just reactions based on the unconscious repetition of earlier patterns that we have learned personally from our parents, groups, experience, and also from the archetypes or patterns within the collective unconscious. This occurs automatically totally outside of our awareness. Our brain's automated function is to compare incoming information to what is familiar. It operates in a very binary fashion analyzing for pattern recognition. Without us having to do anything consciously, it 'turns on' the pattern most like what we are perceiving and we repeat it by default, all without any effort or thought on our part. Highly useful, this automated system keeps us functioning without our having to rethink the thousands of interactions occurring in our day. Negatively it explains why we so often catch ourselves doing something over and over again even when it is not in our best interest. We will be delving into this more deeply in Part II, Chapter Six, as we look at the specifics of the mental level of our field

Looking first at this basic energy structure and its flow factors in a general, layman friendly way gives us a context for beginning a new way of understanding who we are and how we work. Earlier we stated that our Heart Field, like all fields that we know of, is a torus. The dictionary defines a torus as "a doughnut shaped surface generated by a circle rotated about an axis in its plane that does not intersect the circle." See Figure 2 for diagram. For those who may be interested in a very detailed scientific explanation I highly recommend Dr. Claude Swanson's book, <u>The Synchronized Universe, Vol. II: Life Force, The Scientific Basis.</u> He goes into a very thorough exploration of both the history and science of our life force energy, or biofield as it is often called.

For our purposes it is entirely sufficient to have a basic sense of how toroidal flow works and how different aspects of our energy structure are part of it. Seeing the big picture gives us a context in which to locate the chakras, nadis, aura, etheric, and causal layers of our energy structure that takes them out of isolation and helps us see how they are all parts of the whole of our Heart Field. As we'll see the different directional planes of our body/mind/spirit dimensions make it visibly clear that it is only within the heart that they all intersect, and therefore where we are able to access them. Having a basic understanding of our Heart Field as our dynamic energy structure is the first step in becoming able to be aware of and modulate aspects of it consciously in service to our highest good and abundant wellbeing.

4 WHY DOES IT MATTER ?

Within the past half century almost everything we thought we understood about how life works has changed significantly. Nowhere is this truer than in reference to ourselves. While we may become aware of new information, the implications for what it means to us personally and culturally typically lag behind as we process it all. As the rate of information doubling has increased exponentially, our ability to integrate it is challenging.

For a long time we have held the scientific viewpoint that it is possible for us to be separate independent observers. We separated things into subjective and objective; subjective being our own unique individual inner experience, and objective being something real outside of us that everyone shared in common. We looked at material reality as all there is. Even though we now know that we live in an entangled universe where everything is interconnected and interdependent, we continue to use the classical scientific method to verify something as valid. Aware of the limitations of the intellect and reason, we continue to act as if they are our highest human capacity. They are only one half of the whole, and we have been operating on the assumption that they are all of it. It leads us to conclusions which are ultimately erroneous. It also presents us with what we have taken to be duality, when it is the polarity of two halves of a complete cycle.

With ample evidence that energy and information occupy multiple dimensions and that we are made of energy, we require a new perspective in understanding who we are. Our Heart Field includes the multidimensional energy fields that make up the totality of who we are. We have looked at what it is, and covered the basics of how it works from the neutral language of energy. Why does it matter? Who are we? Do we have a purpose, and if so, what is it? These are questions that include the emotional and spiritual dimensions of our heart.

Is there something about human beings that make us unique from other forms of life? Certainly not our DNA as was long thought to be the case in the genetic determinism stream of thought. What a surprise when the long awaited genetic mapping showed that we shared 99% of our DNA with fruit flies. Also that our DNA is not fixed but is dynamic and constantly being altered by our inner and outer environments; both facts refuting what had been taught for decades. So if not genetic superiority, then what is it that makes us stand out?

As one of my psychology professors used to frequently remind us, human beings can only do three things; feel, think, and behave. We contain BOTH light and darkness, positive AND negative, requiring of us CHOICE in our feelings, thoughts and actions. We call this free will, or autonomy and have long thought it a factor unique to humans. Originally we thought we were the only sentient beings, but now it is clear that consciousness occurs at many levels. Cell biologist Candace Pert first recognized and documented this in Molecules of Emotion in 1997, showing that consciousness is present at the level of the individual cell and that with intention we can create our own neurotransmitters, or what are often called the mood chemicals. In 2005, Bruce Lipton followed up her work with Biology of Belief, the research and documentation demonstrating that the biomolecular level of life is determined not by fixed genetics or biochemistry as we thought several decades ago, but at the deeper and primary level by *vibration we experience as feeling*. At the physical level we experience feeling as sensory perception. At the mental level we name it emotion. Both are our perception of energy movement. Biology and medicine are still in the earliest stages of recognizing what physics has accepted for decades; that everything including us is energy and at the most foundational level operates vibrationally.

The second characteristic is choice. Religious traditions have presented moral agency or free will as a unique condition of our humanity, it is attributed to the fact that we are conscious. The recent discovery that consciousness is not limited to humans, but is present in varying degrees in all life forms calls that into question. Now that consciousness is understood as a characteristic of life of all kinds, a new level of understanding is needed to describe what differentiates human consciousness from the consciousness of a cell, a flower, a tree, or an animal. Just as we have categorized life by degrees of movement, and more recently consciousness or awareness, now that we understand consciousness as ubiquitous with life we must refine the differentiation of what it is that makes humans different.

Earlier it was much easier to observe that plants (most of whom have a shorter life span than humans) had a life cycle that included growth from a seed, development, flowering, fruition, decline, and then decay. However, they cannot move, and their action is limited to orienting to the light from wherever they are. Animals have the additional advantage of movement, but seem largely instinctual rather than volitional in their behavior. Thought was— rightly or wrongly—attributed to human beings only. With this mental ability to think came the requirement to make choices.

With the ability to imagine and compare more than one option in response to our condition and setting, we have what theologians and philosophers called free will or moral agency—our behavior is not limited to an instinctual response, but instead we are free to choose not only what to do, but what to think. Implied in this is the ability to perceive more than one option or point of view. This mental ability was attributed to a higher level of development, a more sophisticated level of life, a gift from God. While other life forms seem to operate from a prescribed pattern of being that is confined to a defined cycle with variation coming only in response to environmental conditions related to survival, humans could choose actions both physical and mental which did not necessarily have this direct correlation. In fact it is easy to notice that humans often make choices which seem more destructive than constructive to their life experience. The study of behavior has always intrigued us and has been fodder for poets, muses, and writers as well as philosophers and scientists for as long as we have recorded history.

As medicine became more and more limited to the physical, the non-material aspects of life were ignored with focus on the smaller physical bits of us that our technologies could make visible. With the advent of the electron microscope in the 1960's we could see molecules, and our medicine focused on the molecular and chemical level of how life acts and reacts. Although all other sciences have accepted the vibrational and energy reality for at least half a century, molecular biochemistry remains the basis of our medical diagnosis and treatment still today.

Along with observations limited to the physical world, another basic assumption is that all that impacts life on Earth developed here on the planet Earth over thousands of years of evolution of both the planet and humanity. We now have abundant evidence of Earth's being impacted multiple times by meteors carrying elements that contribute to life, without seriously considering what implications that brings. As our scientific purview continues to expand we now know that not only are there additional galaxies, there are billions of universes. This is an entirely new and much larger framework for humans to contemplate. With the recent discovery that a significant portion of elements that make up our DNA have been identified in a meteor, it raises new questions about our evolution as a species. Are we just from here, or did key elements arrive from elsewhere?

What technology cannot make visible—and thereby real—to us, science ignores. All that it cannot see, by implication becomes irrelevant. Even though every human being experiences consciousness, feelings, emotion, relationships, fear, and love, their reality and impact on our lives is considered inconsequential in scientific investigations. The unstated premise within science is the invisible does not impact the world of matter. The rest of us have a lot of questions about it.

What is love? The question the poets among us have asked for centuries. In one way or another most have expressed the awareness that it is too vast and all-encompassing to define in words, and so have had to settle for describing its aspects and qualities. Love is such a thing. Universal and personal, the driving force behind decisions large and small. To experience it we are happy to forgo many other things.

Love is experienced connection. For decades now that simple expression has, for me, defined love. Although simple, it's the most complete way we can express it in words. It is the reality behind all the flowery expressions of what it looks like, feels like, means to us. Science, at least until very recently, is rarely raised in this endeavor. Yet, when we attempt to explore this most basic of human needs we find there are some very objective things we can say about it, while admitting that all we might say falls short of coming close to what it feels like, what it means to experience it. And that itself is partial proof of the definition. Love is our experience of connection to our Self, to others, and to the Divine. It has already been noted by multiple teachers over the eons of human existence to be everywhere present and the measure of all that we hold dear. People willingly die for love, sacrifice many of life's other pleasures and needs for it, search for it endlessly, and find everything else in life meaningless if it is not accompanied by love.

So what is meant by saying that love is experienced connection? In the scientific world of objective observation and measurement we look to two things, structures and then the relationships to and within them. Both can be described in the universal language of numbers. Mathematical description is clear, succinct, and can make complex relationships visible to us in a brief line of numerical code. We call this a mathematical formula—a recipe for recreating the same structure and relationships for anyone able to read the code and knowing how to express it in material ways. Whether it's an idea or concept we want others to grasp mentally, or the instructions for building a structure, like architectural blueprints for a building, or that little booklet or paper that comes in the box with items telling us how to assemble them, the numbers tell us in what order and positional relationship we are to place the separate parts to create the functional and desired whole object we wish to achieve. In addition to having pieces of the correct size and shape, it is also necessary to place them in proper relationship to each other—at the right angle—to be able to align the small openings in the articulating pieces themselves and allow for this alignment and connection to take place. So even in this most literal and concrete sense we see that relationship to each other and connection are essential aspects of creation.

Of course, when we speak of love we are most often speaking of personal relationships. Whether to nature, art, music or persons, what we love is what we experience ourselves connected to. What we describe as love is actually that experience. What is it we are experiencing when we say we feel love? It is experiencing ourselves more fully, more completely in recognizing the feelings connected with our attachment and relationship to the other. Whether it is nature, animals, art, music, a particular group or person, the sensation is one of belonging, connection, and significance in which we experience ourselves more fully than possible without recognizing that relationship and connection. We experience ourselves as larger than just our self; an essential part of the whole necessary to the nature of what it is.

Some of these experiences are universal, others more unique, yet they all have these same features in common. Their power is so strong that one willingly gives up many of life's other things in order to pursue the object of this experience. While love may be the fabric of the universe, we only perceive it in association with the person, place, or setting in which we have known the feeling previously. We often conclude that it is THAT person, place, or setting that is love, rather than the conductor of what is universally present and available to us. When we fail to realize love for what it is, we most often mistakenly attach it to the object or person with whom we experienced its presence previously and attribute it to that object, rather than knowing that they are not source but conduit for that which is present always everywhere, and that it is our awareness of it which changes. The great teachers have all directed us to Love all. When we perceive ourselves as separate beings we hear this instruction as a challenge to our will; a requirement or test of our devotion or spiritual maturity. It is nothing of the sort. It is shifting our conscious awareness to the dimension in which we are able to know everything and everyone as connected and in relationship. All relationship is in the angles.

We're drowning in a sea of information and not paying any attention to the connections and relationships. How we connect the information creates beliefs. It is the beliefs that create meaning for us in our lives. What we think the information means determines our choices (or just makes them automatically for us according to previous patterns if we're not paying attention). Our choices determine our feelings, attitudes and behavior. The crucial factor is the connections we make. Almost no one is paying attention to this –except the marketing folks; who do this very well. They make the connections for us to make the result they want they want seem the reasonable one. As long as we are only paying attention to the information itself, the connections remain powerfully subconscious. It's the connections that create the beliefs for making the choice.

We spend far too much time in therapy focusing on the information or event, when the only thing that really matters is the connections; the relationship. All of our myriad techniques focus on following the thread of either thoughts or events as if it were they that are the problem. When it is the connections—the relationship—that give those experiences meaning to the particular person and become dysfunctional when they create an ineffective pattern of choices and behavior. It is also unique to that person and type of situation, which is why we can have someone who is normal in most areas of life and totally dysfunctional in one particular area where bad connections have been made.

It is why effective therapy—no matter the particular process— follows the connections until the client becomes conscious of the pattern they've created. As soon as they see the relationship they are able to make new connections, but not before. This includes relationships between Body/Mind/Spirit. It's difficult to be healthy (coherent) in one level when not in the others. This shows up at both ends of the spectrum of wellness; our natural state. It is equally true for the morbidly obese, the psychotic, the spiritual illiterate AND those who are perfectionistic, obsessively attentive to physical beauty or strength, mentally addicted to ideas and thought, or spiritually focused to the degree that other aspects of life are deemed unimportant. They all lack coherence, which is comparable development of all levels and the ability to discern and use them all equally well in response to the requirements of a particular situation.

What do points of connection do? They direct our focus. They determine where we end up by showing us exactly where we change direction from just forward momentum to a change of degree that takes us in a new direction. Each interchange provides this alteration of forward direction. Even a slight change at any one takes us to a completely different end point. When multiplied by multiple connecting points, we end up in entirely different places than we would have if those connections were different.

Why does it matter what the Heart Field is or how it works? It's not about another fact or theory to add onto what we already have. It's certainly not something new; it's been in front of us forever. It completely replaces our old limited way of seeing and gives us new glasses, a bigger framework, an infinite perspective to see more clearly than before. Everything looks different. We see a different picture that tells a different story. What was blurry and indistinct now comes into focus. What is the primary shift it points to? The shift from either this or that, to this and that. From arguing over which half of a cycle is real to realizing that both are necessary when we enlarge the map enough to see the whole. The shift from false self to True Self, from separate to union and unique perspective, from masculine to feminine leadership, from transcendent Divinity to embodied spirit. It's not just different content. It is also a different process.

There really is only one question we ever need to ask. Are we coming from love or fear?

Sometimes it's a bit confusing because there is some of both. It's more a continuum rather than an either /or. Like everything, it's a both/and. But what is useful to us in the asking is that it shifts our perspective to the authentic question, are you looking from the inside or out? From the head or the heart? The external world shows us one picture—of separation, discrete individuals and objects; situations seem unconnected. Threats abound and we need to protect ourselves. We can't do what our hearts are calling us to because we need to focus on making money. We need money because we can't live in the world without it. One step at a time we find entirely rational reasons why we have to live from the world's story. Each step takes us further from our feelings. We learn over time not to trust them. Eventually the shift is complete and we live and make our choices in alignment with external decrees. We have no sense that it is we who are creating the reality by our compliance to it. On the larger human scale it is the false self of the world, the mental part of the collective without the heart. Just as we individually must each expand our consciousness beyond mind separated from heart to the larger Heart Field where we get an entirely different picture, the world cannot change until enough individual people shift their perspective to the internal vastness of the heart as their primary compass. Just as for each of us it shifts everything, it will shift everything in the world, but its occurrence depends upon each of us doing our part, making that shift. When enough of us do, we will change the world. We will tell a different story. We will make different choices. There will be different results.

It seems so daunting a task, almost impossible really, that we tend to not even make the effort; and yet that is exactly what is needed. It can't happen without us. With each small individual choice made from love instead of fear, another drop flows into a new archetype. We create one small instance of love made visible, even if it seems that no one will see it or notice it. We don't do it to produce a certain result. We do it because it is the authentic expression of love. That's all. When this internal motivation is present it isn't dependent on the result. Being love is enough. The example is always before us. It is how the Divine always is with us. Just like God is always present Love in our lives whether or not we notice, we can be Love wherever we are whether or not anyone notices. It still is Love present in that moment in that place with that person. We are not responsible to create a particular result. We are just called to be the Love. We may or may not ever even see or know the results. It doesn't matter. Ours is to be the embodied spirit; God's hands in the world. Just as our hands are extensions of our heart, each of us are the hands of God, the expression of God's heart.

Why the Heart Field matters isn't that it adds another concept or technique or modality to our tool box. It is that it changes our whole worldview. It fundamentally shifts our perspective to a new and higher vantage point from which we see and understand our self and all else differently. It shifts our identity. Heart Centered Wellness™ isn't another health model. It is whole different perspective on what health and wellness is. It includes the spiritual as the essential foundation. It frees us from the broken and false narrative we are immersed in and provides us a new perspective from which to see all the interwoven aspects of our lives as a synchronized whole. To see the connection and relationship of one part to another. To realize that every choice affects all of who we are in some ways, and that it doesn't just affect us. Our choices, our way of being, ripples out and alters others and the environment around us. We have no way of seeing the effects it might have, and we don't need to. In being the presence of love in the moment at that spot, we manifest its reality. Its presence may remind others of its reality and inspire them to be love too. The pay it forward movement is a good example. Something as simple as doing a small good deed like paying for someone's coffee has brightened the day of both the giver and receiver. That ripples out to others who perhaps just observed it and it reminds them that they too can do the same. It reassures us of the power and reality of love. It feels so good for the very reason that it is in alignment with who we really are. It changes everything. We feel it. It feels great.

We are energized.

So we don't need to see the big picture or understand how it works, we just need to do the one small thing in front of us, make the one small choice of being loving and follow it up with the action of doing. That's all. Then we can smile and go on our way. That's how we change ourselves that's how we change the world. It's heart centered wellness and abundant living. It is abundant due to its multiplier effect. What we send out both ripples to others and also returns to us multiplied. It doesn't get any better than that.

As Claude Swanson reminds us in <u>Life Force Energy: The Scientific Basis</u>, the evidence for some of the earliest applications for torsion and subtle energy are thousands of years old, and found in stone megaliths all over the world. He says its use to control the Earth energies, as well as maintain health in the body, may be the oldest technology on the planet.

We have to own the spiritual. It is not religion, it is the essence, the highest of who we are. It IS our True Self. We can't be one and not own the other; they are the same thing.

The Heart Field

PART II

ACCESSING OUR HEART FIELD

The Heart Field

.

5 PHYSICAL FACTORS

Once we understand what the Heart Field is and how it works it is clear that for optimal function its energies at every level need to be able to flow smoothly without obstruction or disconnection. This is true within each level, between each level, and between our Heart Field and the outer environment. In Part II we will examine the particular factors that affect our energy integrity within each level, and then in Part III, between each level within and without.

Our physical body is the densest energetic level of who we are, and perhaps for that reason the easiest to start with. There are multiple factors that affect its ability to function well. Looking at our bodies from an energy viewpoint presents a very different picture than the one we are used to looking at it from the current cultural or medical perspective. Let's put on a different pair of glasses to see more clearly what promotes healthy energy transmission and a healthy physical body.

The Body:

Life energy is never still, its hallmark is motion. At a very literal level all our efforts are about presence and navigation. Being present physically is dependent upon our body. To a great extent our possibilities of navigation rest heavily on our body, its structure, its capabilities, its condition, fuel quality and quantity. Most of the basics are already familiar to each of us, but let's look at them from a Heart Field perspective.

A very popular book over the past decade has been Dr. Bruce Lipton's <u>Biology of Belief</u>. A cell biologist, Lipton has made the biology of the body interesting and easy to understand, while also validating the impact of the vibrational environment on cell behavior. The vibrational environment, or frequency, is what we perceive in our body as sensory feelings. This is a radical departure from the biomolecular view of biology we had been used to. It completely turns on its head most of the underlying assumptions about how our bodies work and is entirely congruent with Heart Field theory. Basically he presents our body as a community of fifty trillion cells, and states that each of our cells is always in one of two modes: growth or defense. To the degree our cells need to defend they are not available for growth. The factors that determine which of these two modes our cells are in are located in the inner and outer cell environment and are vibrational. In other words, the feelings you have determine the cells' growth or defense status. These feelings include both physical sensation and the mental overlay of interpretation often called emotion. Together they present a frequency harmonic of vibration within and around the cell that alter its function.

For those of you who may want to delve more deeply into the physical in an intensely scientific way there is no better place to start than Mae-Wan Ho's 1998 book titled, <u>The Rainbow and the Worm: The Physics of Organisms</u>. She describes our bodies as 'a bag of liquid crystal,' and proposes that our crystalline nature could account for properties of pattern formation and even our faculties of consciousness. Dr. Ho presents biological effects of electromagnetic fields, research into biophotons in relation to energy mobilization, each of our cells as individual tensegrity units, and quotes Ervin Lazlo's book, <u>The Interconnected Universe</u>, as offering the possibility that the liquid crystalline continuum of the body may be a quantum holographic medium.

For readers more interested in practical application we can start by simplifying the above paragraph, with apologies to Mae-Wan Ho, by saying that one function of the skin (our largest organ) is to serve as a container for all of the component parts of our physical body. Because all of the structures of our body are crystalline, and the largest part of our mass is water, we are piezoelectric or good conductors of energy. Bearing in mind that life energy operates vibrationally, through harmonic frequency alterations on a moment to moment basis broadcast by our heartbeat, our bodies are ideally composed to function by resonant communication. We communicate by frequency vibrations. Moreover, resonance travels much faster than the electrical impulses of our nervous system, allowing the whole body to instantaneously receive information needed to operate as a unified whole. This basic energy vantage point allows us to recognize two foundational components of our physical function, grounding and water. Let's look at each of them in relation to the integrity of the physical aspects of our Heart Field.

Grounding:

As humbling as it may be to realize that we share some energy attributes with machinery, our modern lifestyle has resulted in something humans didn't have to think about prior to the last half century. Many are still unaware of its role in maintaining our physical health, as its negative effects only gradually grew into our awareness as a likely contribution to many of our health problems over the past two decades. It is grounding. Anyone who operates any type of electrical machinery knows that it must be grounded to operate safely. It might work for a while if not grounded, but eventually can build up a charge imbalance that causes malfunction or even equipment failure. Understanding the piezoelectric quality of our body's structure allows us to see that we share this in common.

Up until perhaps the 1950's, human beings spent quite a lot of their time outdoors in nature. Either barefoot or in natural leather soled shoes, contact with the Earth created a ground that easily discharged whatever free radicals (read electrons) our bodily processes created. It was not something we had to pay attention to, or even be aware of. Living in alignment with nature kept us energetically balanced. As our industrial and technological proficiency developed, modern conveniences changed our lifestyles in significant ways. Change in itself is neutral, but with all change comes both positive and negative potentials. While we are grateful for the positives, it sometimes takes a while to become aware of the impact of the negatives. This was the case with grounding. Free radicals have now been implicated as major factors in most of the chronic illnesses that have been increasing at alarming rates. When we are not grounded we have no way to discharge these excess electrons and they then create the inflammation underlying all of our chronic diseases.

Several changes cumulatively contributed to our regular disconnection from the Earth. The advent of air conditioning, like heating systems before it, kept us inside when weather conditions were unfavorable. Leather shoes were replaced first with rubber soled shoes, now entire shoes made out of non-conductive manmade materials. Our homes progressively included less natural, and more manmade components like vinyl siding and composite chemical products like carpeting and flooring. Completely unintentional, our modern advances separated us from our connection to Mother Earth. It took a while to notice that the rapid increase in poor health overall might be connected. In fact, it took a TV lineman to make the connection, and then a decade after that before he could get an MD or scientist to investigate his findings.

In what is now commonly known as earthing, people are choosing to return to natural materials like hardwood flooring, clothing made out of organic fibers, leather shoes or earthing shoes that incorporate metal conductive plugs, and bedsheets and conductive pads that can be connected to the grounding hole in electrical outlets. Of course the best, easiest, and free option is to spend about an hour each day outside with your feet on the ground, but it's nice to have alternatives available for when that isn't practical. With free radicals medically indicted as a primary cause of inflammation, and inflammation now the recognized underlying factor in every chronic disease including heart disease, diabetes, arthritis, hardening of the arteries and high blood pressure, it would be a major step in improving health for everyone to become aware of the importance of grounding and to take whichever steps work for them to make it a daily reality.

Water

Along with air to breathe—the next topic—water is the most essential need of our human bodies. Covering the largest part of the Earth, and making up the largest part of our body, water has multiple functions contributing to our physical wellbeing. Some are more commonly understood than others. Hydration is generally realized to be important as a transportation vehicle in many of the body's systems for instance. Less well known is that vibrations resonate farther and more rapidly in water than in air, making our liquid inner environment a conducive conductor of our heartbeats' harmonic frequencies. Some cutting edge research is suggestive that water may also serve as an information storage battery; an intriguing idea that is aligned with somatic memory theories of emotional trauma. New and still controversial issues related to water involve its structure. In biochemistry which is the medical standard, water is always H_2O. The actual structure of H_2O isn't addressed. This is beginning to change, and changes the question from not only how much water do we need, but what kind of water serves our optimal health?

A few years ago the late Masaru Emoto captivated the world with his incredible photographs of the crystalline structure of water. Captured in the brief transitional state between liquid and frozen, the crystals were either beautifully symmetrical or distorted and contorted depending upon the environment they were in as they were freezing. This was not only true at the level of biochemistry; for instance if the water was pure or polluted. The results were the same in response to sound waves of music; beautiful crystals formed with classical and harmonic music, while heavy metal or dissonant sounds created ugly distorted crystals. More astounding still, emotion itself affected the crystals. Whether written as words on the container or sent as intentions from the heart, the effect on the crystal formation was definitive. Words and intentions of love, beauty, truth, and compassion created beautiful crystals, while ones like anger, hate, and malice formed crystals as distorted as those found in toxic waste water. Emoto's photographs visually demonstrate an energy pattern retention in the water's structure that aligns with homeopathic principles and is starting to be borne out with acclaimed scientific evidence.

The late Dr Rustum Roy at Pennsylvania State University worked extensively with structured water as a healing agent. In a more recent work, The Fourth Phase of Water by Dr. Gerald H. Pollack, which received the NIH Director's Award for Transformational scientific investigation, Pollack presents a simple foundation for understanding how changes in water structure underlie most energy transitions of both form and motion on Earth. Mae-Wan Ho calls it the most important scientific discovery of the century. Since our bodies, like the Earth, are made up mostly of water, emerging understanding of and attention to water structure are becoming an important aspect of physical wellness.

So what practical information does this give us in regard to water?

Some basic guidelines allow you to integrate these water principles easily at home:

1. <u>How much water do we need to be adequately hydrated</u>? An easy rule of thumb is half your body weight in ounces each day. Ideally this is consumed frequently in small amounts throughout the day. This allows our metabolic functions to operate within a continuous state of balance rather than large swings of fluid overload and then deprivation. The amount of course can be adjusted up or down by increased heat and activity, or health issues like kidney function problems.

2. <u>How can I alter the structure of the water to maximize its health benefits?</u>
   There are a number of water systems available commercially that purport to structure your water for you, but there are some very simple things you can do to alter the structure of your water yourself for free.
   a. With bottled water found at work and events, you can just vigorously shake the bottle for 30-60 seconds. This clears energy patterns already present like an energy practitioner might clear your energy field. Then you can place your hands around the bottle, focus your mental attention on the water and from your heart send an intention for love, wellness, or whatever you may wish with the power of the intensity of your feeling for about a minute. As Emoto's photographs showed, this literally changes the structure of the water and as you drink it, you are placing into your inner environment the beautiful holographic structures of wellness.
   b. Another way you can convert water structure at home is with what I call "blue glass water." The frequency of the color blue is water's ideal natural state, and so placing water in a blue bottle and allowing it to sit where there is light going through it for a short while is an easy way to restructure it.

c.   In addition to the blue glass, you can paint or tape a written word on the outside of your glass water bottle. You can place it near a source of harmonious music. You can place it in direct sunlight for 30-60 minutes.

Any of these simple steps can be used to create your own structured water. Taken in adequate amounts throughout the day, because it is such an essential factor to so many bodily functions that we know of and others we are just beginning to discover, water is a basic element of physical wellness. Because our Heart Field works through vibration or frequency, having a well hydrated body of harmonically structured water contributes immensely to the integrity and clear communication it can offer us.

Breath

Along with water, oxygen is our body's other essential need. I often joke with students when discussing Maslow's hierarchy of needs that no matter how highly developed a person is, they return to the first step of 'survival' usually in 30 seconds or less by merely placing one hand over their mouth and holding their nose closed with the other. I do this not for entertainment, but to make the point visible that our lives are dynamic and at any moment we can switch from one state to another. It also offers a clear demonstration of the priority of breath to our physical body. At the physical level of our Heart Field breath serves several functions.

Because it's such a basic life function our breathing operates automatically most of the time, and the fullness of our breath is related to the body's need for oxygen. Except for when we are doing some strenuous activity or are stressed, we probably only use a third to half of our lung capacity most of the time. Since oxygen is a key element in our metabolic processes, most of our inactive time when we are breathing automatically is spent in less than optimal oxygenation of our blood. A little recognized fact about aerobic exercise is that a large percentage of its value is that the muscle demand for oxygen while exercising strenuously causes us to take full deep breaths, providing much more oxygen to our red blood cells with each breath. This enhances mental clarity, energy levels, and all around metabolic function. You can actually receive much of the benefit of aerobic exercise by just doing full, slow, and deep breathing. All your body tissues and organs receive full oxygenation with every complete breath, allowing them optimal metabolic function.

We also have the choice to breathe with awareness or attention, directing both the rate and depth of each breath. Yoga traditions have recognized and used a variety of intentional breath patterns called pranayama to intentionally alter both mental and physical states. Native and other traditions also use what is called element breathing which correlates nose and mouth breathing patterns with the four elements of Earth, water, air, and fire. They also use breath as an access to spiritual states.

In Western culture the power of breath to alter our stress response through biofeedback and autogenic training has been known since mid-twentieth century. First, Elmer Green at Menninger Clinic did early work with biofeedback, documenting our ability to alter our temperature, blood pressure, and other physical parameters using breath and mental focus. Dr. C Norman Shealy advanced these concepts even further in the development of autogenic training and many other holistic bioenergy practices. We will cover breath in much more detail in its role as the first step of meditation later on, but here it is important to note its physical role in blood oxygenation and its intentional directed use to energize or relax our nervous system response.

Practical applications of breath are easy using the four element method:

1. All breaths start with a complete breath. Sit in an erect posture with spine straight and shoulders relaxed to allow for full expansion of the lungs. Beginning with exhalation, contract your abdominal muscles to completely empty your lungs. Then relax the abdomen to begin the inhalation, and allow the lungs to slowly fill completely. At the top of the inhalation you can expand the top of the lungs a bit more by just continuing to inhale intentionally without straining. Try to make your inhalation and exhalation about the same length. Breathing as slowly, deeply, evenly, and completely as possible in this manner fully oxygenates your body. Just doing this for one to three minutes causes the relaxation response to switch on; a good antidote to stress.

2. Earth breath – this breath works just like it sounds; it grounds us. Using the full breath above breathe in and out through the nose. Place both feet on the floor uncrossed. Hands can rest on the thighs either up or down, but with fingers open. This is a useful breath to do for a few minutes whenever you are feeling scattered, anxious, or having difficulty concentrating.

3. Water breath – is a cooling and healing breath. Again using full breath, breathe in through the nose and out through the mouth. This is a soothing, calming breath useful for bringing an immediate cooling effect both physically and mentally. It's a good breath to use when overwhelmed, angry, impatient, or needing to let go of something.

4. Air breath – is a good breath to use when you want to stimulate your creativity, imagination, and freedom from confines of whatever sort. Air breath is done breathing in and out through the mouth.

5. Fire breath – is an energizing breath. Opposite of water breath, with fire breath you breathe in through the mouth

and out through the nose. This is a warming and stimulating breath useful when you are feeling sluggish, slow, low energy.

One aspect of breathing that is obvious, but not usually noticed is that it is one of two major methods through which we exchange the external environment and the internal. The other is nutrition and excretion which we'll address shortly. In terms of our breath, the exchange is less material and therefore often overlooked. Spiritual teachings refer to God breathing the breath of life into humankind. It was understood as the animating force or spirit that made the physical being alive. As we grow to understand ourselves more and more as energetically entangled participants in the Living Matrix, we come to understand one quality of breath as a frequency exchange between our inner and outer environments. We breathe in the air and frequencies of our immediate environment, its frequencies become altered by the harmonics of our feelings, and we exhale, returning to the environment our contribution to its positive or negative nature.

Nutrition

At its most basic, our food is our body's fuel supply. Most of us would never think of putting low grade fuel in our cars and expect them to run well, but our relationship with food is so much more complicated. We eat not only to provide our body the fuel it needs, but also as a social activity, for emotional reasons, when we are bored, etc. There is so much constant information about food, much of it offering conflicting advice, that it can be a challenge to know what and how much your body needs for health and wellness.

Add to that marketing propaganda, frequently changing governmental and medical guidelines, and too many books to count on this diet or that diet and most of us feel confused at best. Many just give up entirely and stop paying attention at all. Probably more common is the yoyo syndrome in which we alternate between some strict regimen which works temporarily but leaves out some significant food groups, and then returning to our old habits as the limitations create a rebound effect of cravings. Our country's staggering obesity epidemic and related health problems are crippling our healthcare system in a cycle of rapidly declining health, and highlight the failures of our food supply industry.

Seemingly unrelated factors also have a significant effect. Our lives have become busier and filled with more activities, making us susceptible to convenience rather than quality as a high food priority. The suburbs or bedroom communities that sprang up last half century partnered with individual car ownership as the norm to change our lifestyles in ways promoted as improvements which have had just the opposite effect on our body's healthy functioning. Fast food became the answer to lunch and dinner on the run. As we got accustomed to it, breakfast was added. Pesticides, hormones, and antibiotics were added to increase productivity, plants were genetically modified, and in just a few short decades created an industry in which our food often bears little resemblance to its natural state. So many large vested interests now control our food supply and are spending millions to keep us from even knowing what is in our food, that it now takes real attention and intention to provide the real food our body needs. Many groups are now providing advocacy status and readily available information and updating on related particulars, and their efforts at public education are starting to have effect.

Surprisingly, there is really very little you need to know to provide healthy nutrition. First it bears remembering what the fuel is we are taking in with our food. What is the fuel that keeps our bodies healthy and energized? Stored light or photons. We have all been taught that plants convert sunlight through a process called photosynthesis, taking in carbon dioxide and giving off oxygen. While correct, this focus on the environmental effects doesn't really tell the whole story. We have previously said that photons are the smallest units of life that we know of and appear to us as frequency ranges of light we see as color. Inherent in plants is the propensity to take in and store certain light frequencies and informational patterns. This gives a particular plant its color and shape. Increasingly dieticians are advising their clients to eat a rainbow of colors of foods, knowing this will provide the full range of needed light frequencies to fuel all the body's needs.

Meat also has a role. Animals also provide fuel as stored light. They eat the plants, then we eat the stored light in the meat. This as many point out is a very costly and inefficient way to get our light fuel, but may have originally served as source during seasons or weather which did not readily offer plant availability.

Sunlight itself is our most obvious source of photons. Our skin cells, like all of our cells both take in and give off photons. We are familiar with its ability to absorb Vitamin D, essential to a number of body processes, but perhaps less aware that it is the actual fuel that our energy body requires to support and maintain life. Some groups in the US, following in the footsteps of some spiritual traditions, actually eat no food at all, and claim to get all their nutrition from sun gazing. This can be a dangerous practice if not properly trained, so I'm not recommending it; just pointing it out as verification that our essential fuel source is biophotons.

For readers wanting to eat a healthy diet the following few guidelines are all that's necessary.

1. Eat real food. That is food that is alive. Simple as that is, in today's world it requires definition. Real food is organically grown, non-GMO, and intact or whole in form. Fake food, or processed products that look and taste like food, but really are altered or even synthetic imitations can't be used by our body efficiently. Because our body's needs are not being met, we remain hungry and end up consuming much more. As the medical establishment struggles with the health fallout of a culture of obesity, large economic interests spend obscene amounts of money keeping this information from the general public. Medical professionals and registered dieticians alike get far too much of their information from the prevailing industry and little education of the need for whole foods.

2. Locally grown within one hundred miles. This addresses your body's need for what is in season where you live, and mitigates against long travel times diminishing its nutritional value by either being picked unripe or losing freshness en route. Eating what is in season honors our body's needs for different foods at different times. For example, when I pay attention to what my body wants I'm drawn to fresh fruits and vegetables and light clear beverages in the warmer weather and warm more substantial moist foods in colder weather. Most communities are fortunate enough to have weekly farmer's markets or farm stands that both supply fresh food and allow you to support your local economy at the same time.

3. Aim to eat foods of every color of the rainbow. This offers a balance of nutrients that support the different needs of the body. Eating whole foods also provides the fiber and absorption rate that facilitate healthy gut function and prevents blood sugar spikes that occur when we alter its form substantially.

4. Eat what your body is hungry for. Learn to listen to your body's signals of when you need to eat and what type of food you are hungry for. Studies of small children offered

a full variety of foods showed that over a week they would choose a balanced diet. Sadly we quickly socialize that out in a number of ways, but we can quickly learn to pay attention again. In my counseling experience with clients it seems to take between five to twenty one days to reorient ourselves. Initially you may overload on one type of food, usually one you commonly try to limit. For example you may eat a lot of chocolate, ice cream, or chips for the first few days. Then when you realize you can have whatever you want any time, your body starts to desire what it actually needs.

5. Finally, apply the 80/20 rule. It's not practical or useful to become a fanatic. Circumstances and occasions occur that make the above guidelines difficult for a variety of reasons. If you apply them 80% of the time, you will still end up with what you need for good health. As you reconnect with your body's feelings it will guide you and in the process make eating a celebration of joy rather than another area of stress.

Exercise

If there is anything we obsess about as much as food in our health practices, it's exercise. We have made what was just a natural part of living into an entire industry. Beginning with the industrial age, more occupations moved from out in nature to enclosed buildings. But work was still largely physical. As the industrial age transitioned into the age of technology, we added sedentary to being indoors in artificially controlled environments. Gradually over time our bodies got less and less active as a natural part of our daily life. We spend less and less time in nature. A pretty typical daily schedule for a large percentage of our population might look something like: get up, get dressed and out the door in less than an hour, drive to work, sit at a desk for eight hours, drive home, sit in front of a TV or other tech device for several hours of news, social catch up, and entertainment, go to bed.

We are all familiar with the old cliché, "Use it or lose it." This is certainly true for our body as well as mind and spirit. Life exists to be lived, and those dimensions we don't use gradually atrophy and eventually don't work at all. Work, which really means useful activity, gradually changed its social meaning from challenging and significant, to something to be avoided if possible. This was particularly true for physical work which became demoted to a status of less social value than mental work. We were advised to 'work smart, not hard,' and it became a sign of superior human status in the larger culture. Over time the labels of white collar and blue collar jobs created yet another separation between us.

As we started to experience the cumulative effects of our general inactivity, physical decline, we created artificial ways to maintain our physical conditioning. We cast iron into weights, complete with labeling to show how much we could lift. Machines were invented that duplicated the natural moments of walking, running, and climbing. First treadmills, then stair steppers, spinning, and elliptical machines provided a similar motion training for our muscles without the 'inconvenience' of being out in nature. A multibillion dollar industry was created to provide work without work. Scientific analysis worked out very specific amounts of time and intensity needed in a particular exercise to get a particular result. Today we find ourselves wearing monitoring devices to give us instant feedback and reminders of when to move. Owning one has become a social status symbol. Elite athletes go further, some even using steroids to sculpt their physique into an exaggerated caricature of its natural beauty and enhance their temporary performance at the price of their long term health.

I hope that last paragraph sounds as ridiculous as it is. How did we get to a place where ordinary physical activity was removed from its natural place as an integral part of living? Even the experts who measure these things have noted that, taken out of context, running on a treadmill is not the same physical experience as running outside in nature.

In this context the same underlying thread of separation from what is natural is the clue that leads us to the answer of what is actually needed. It is unrealistic to think that going backwards is either practical or desirable. Although life goes in cycles, change is the one constant and it never repeats. We are not going to return to nature as it was in older times. Some groups have tried this with little success. As we become more holistic in our thinking and begin to perceive that we are composed of holographic light patterns manifesting in form, fractal unfolding demonstrates the pattern of our energy movement. Just skip that last sentence if that's jumping a dimension too far ahead.

The question before us is what physical activity do we need to promote health and wellbeing? The answer can be summed up in one statement. Just move most of the sixteen hours a day that you are awake. It doesn't really matter all that much what you do, just move. Exercise from a holistic standpoint isn't meant to be an activity set apart. It's just movement as a part of whatever daily activities we are engaged in. It feels wonderful to move our body. Just pay attention to what feels joyful to you and do that. Make every activity of your day an opportunity for feeling the physicality of what you are engaged in and gratitude for the experience of embodied spirit that you are. You may be pleasantly surprised to discover just how energizing this attention and appreciation of our body is.

The previous paragraph is actually entirely sufficient, but for those readers who like more specificity, or need some instruction to make the transition to this new perspective of physical wellbeing a reality, some simple practices can include:

1. Instead of sitting while watching TV, walk about the room or do some simple dance steps. You might start out doing this during every commercial break, and see what happens.

2. Just like you brush your teeth every day, you can brush your energy field. Using your fingers like a comb, just comb through from head to feet several times all around. Shake off your hands every couple of strokes. This clears your energy field of any tangles or obstructions just like combing your hair does. You can also just brush over your body with your hands in the same manner, starting with the face and over the head, then down the neck, shoulders and arms, down the front and back of the torso, then down the front, back, and sides of the legs to the feet. End by rising up on your toes and letting your heels drop sharply six or seven times. This resets your normal energy balance after you have cleared it.

3. Similar to what we did with water to clear its structure, you can just stand and shake all over for a minute or two. Although it looks a bit silly, it's actually fun and you may find yourself adding the benefit of laughter and positive neurotransmitter production to your energy clearing. Add a jump or two or the heel drop noted in #2 at the end to reset your natural energy balance and increase your lymphatic circulation.

4. Spinning like a whirling dervish can be useful when we have either an excess or deficiency of energy. To bring in more energy use your left foot as a pivot and spin counterclockwise with right arm extended, creating a centripetal vortex. To release excess energy, do just the opposite. Pivoting on the right foot spinning clockwise with left arm extended creates a centrifugal vortex spinning out excess energy. If you look at your extended hand while spinning and put both hands together palms facing your

face for several seconds when you stop you won't lose your balance.

5. A few stretches interspersed in doing household activities or getting in and out of the car offer added benefit without the need to find more time in your day. Switching our usual driving behavior from cruising the parking lot to find a spot closest to the door, to intentionally parking a bit further out and using the cruise time to walk a few more steps and breathe a few more breaths of fresh air provide more physical exercise and is also mentally refreshing.

6. Take five minutes before breakfast, at lunch, or after dinner to go outside and just enjoy several full breaths of fresh air and sunshine. Even these very brief intervals will reconnect you with nature and realign your energy system in positive ways.

Rest

As I hope you are starting to notice, all of life occurs in cycles of expansion and contraction of various sorts and lengths. On the physical level this is cycles of activity and rest. Most have heard of our circadian rhythm, the two hour rotation of cycles of our various organ systems over a twenty four hour day. Research has noted the imbalance in our hormonal production, fertility rates, and other factors when the normal rotation of sleep during night hours and activity during the daytime are interrupted on a regular basis. Even short interruptions like a long flight result in jet lag, our body needing a period of adjustment before it is back in balance. With a century long history of gradually increasing environmental alteration our natural rhythms are now frequently distressed.

Just as the seasons offer differing proportions of daylight and darkness, our body's need for rest is not the set eight hours often given. It too varies with many factors affecting what is needed.

The eight hour, one third of the day formula is the current operational model, perhaps developed as artificial environments and many more options of activity resulted in people getting less and less sleep. Quite a bit of public attention is now starting to be paid to airline pilots, truck drivers, doctors and nurses, and others whose professional capabilities are substantially compromised by inadequate rest. We do know that our sleep pattern requires ninety minutes for a full cycle. That means that if you awaken at the end of a ninety minute cycle you will likely feel alert and ready to function, while if in the middle of a cycle, groggy and a bit slow.

How many sleep cycles we need in a twenty four hour day, or if it's better to have them altogether or at several intervals throughout the day remains an unanswered question. I suspect there are also seasonal variations, perhaps needing more in the cold and dark of winter and less in the warmth and extended daylight of summer. It will also vary according to your health status, age, and other personal factors. As you learn more and more to listen and trust the feeling messages your body is constantly giving you, your inner guidance over outside experts, you will quickly realize that giving yourself permission to honor your physical needs is a reliable way to maintaining physical health.

The spiritual aspect of our physical being has been viewed quite differently by different traditions through the ages. From the physical body as illusory, to considering it of base and impure nature needing to be controlled, to thinking it irrelevant to spiritual concerns, the patriarchal one sided transcendental dominance of worldviews for the past several thousand years has not given the physical a place of importance. As the post shift matrilineal consciousness again emerges, the physical body is understood as the other half and integral part of the whole cycle of descent and return. Transcendence and immanence are two halves of the same cycle. We are embodied spirit. Christ consciousness is not about worshipping the messenger, but rather accepting the message he came to deliver at the beginning of the last age. We are embodied divinity just as the man Jesus modeled for us and taught in his words two thousand years ago. "The kingdom of God is within you." Luke 17:21. Not specific to just Christianity but a reality within all of us eternally awaiting our remembrance, immanence or embodying divine spirit is the other half of the cycle in which the transcendent divine descends into expression in form and then turns to complete the cycle of ascendance and return. It is the feminine principle of the heart. Richard Rohr recently put it this way, "Incarnation means embodiment, enfleshment. The spiritual world is revealed in the material world. We must take Immanence to its logical conclusion."

As the densest energy level of the multidimensional human being, our physical body is the manifest expression of spirit in form. As we give loving attention to our physical needs and intentional expression, we honor a higher reality of experience. We move beyond previous evolutionary stages of focus on physical survival and the mental development of cognition and reason. As we learn to expand our consciousness to the level of our Heart Field we evolve to the higher level of intuition and the dimensional intersection of access to all the levels that comprise our full human being.

6 MENTAL FACTORS

"The intuitive mind is a sacred gift, and the rational mind is a faithful servant. We have created a society that honors the servant and has forgotten the gift."   ---Albert Einstein

Thoughts are energy, just as our bodies are energy. The mental realm is the intermediary layer between our physical self and our spiritual self. Our physical self is finite manifest reality. Our spiritual self is infinite essence reality; the I AM we were before we had a face as the ancients would say. We are conscious mentally and able to conceptualize and reflect with our brains about who we are and why we are here.

There has been no more active dimension of our Heart Field over the last five thousand years than our mental function. Our thinking layer is often called 'mind' and while this is partially true, our mental function is actually only one half of our full mind. Too many still think of mind as emerging from our brains, rather than the more accurate statement, our brain function is one part of our mind. Mind is not produced there, it is just the level of consciousness humanity grew into over the just ended evolutionary period. It was the part of us under most development in the last evolutionary age of human beings, and so not surprising that many are still languishing in it as if it were the dominant feature of our humanity and our highest human function. Even though we have stepped into a new age, the implications are still largely unrecognized and many are still brain focused in their efforts to diagnose and analyze human health and wellbeing. In paraphrasing another Einstein quote, a problem can't be solved at the level in which it was created.

In looking at the dimensions of our Heart Field and how to access them, the most familiar to us is our mental function. For the past five thousand years or so it has been humanity's developmental task to expand our brain function from the purely instinctual reptilian brain, to the mid-brain with its emotional and short-term memory capacities, then to the higher abstract reasoning functions of the cerebral cortex. From an evolutionary purview we are aware that early humans' primary focus was on survival in the physical world. Once that became relatively stable we began to explore our minds, our intellect and the faculty of reason. On a collective scale this is similar to the pattern of individual human growth and development. The first stage of life is spent growing and developing physically, the next on brain and mental development, then in adulthood we grow into realization of our spiritual essence. Each stage has a whole new dimension but also includes all of what came before. During the just ended age, the mental realm has been the primary arena of human awareness. In this model, humanity is just finishing its collective adolescence. Perhaps that explains much of the behavior we see.

Functionally we have two brains; the left and right hemispheres operating differently in binary fashion and connected through a central link called the corpus callosum. The left brain works in a linear manner and is responsible for rational thinking. It is useful in step by step logical analysis. The right brain is more spatial, creative, and holistic. The brain works somewhat like a computer. The brain is the hardware and the software is made up of an accumulation of what we have been taught by our parents, culture, religion, and personal experience. There is also evidence which suggests that collective memories of our lineage are also stored. It used to be thought that memories are stored in our brains, however the newest science points toward somatic body memory storage, with the brain collating them when released and presenting the reconstructed picture as a whole memory. Heart Field storage is also a possibility. It has also been noted that male and female brains work differently with many more brain areas turning on in a given activity in females. There is still much to learn in this area.

The computer analogy is fairly useful. The automatic default option is always operational but can be redirected with attention and intention. As a highly effective timesaver, whenever a new event, thought, or perception enters the brain as it does thousands of times every day, it uses its binary code pattern recognition to quickly identify which pattern the incoming information most closely resembles and then automatically turning on that software program. It's why we so often find ourselves repeating old patterns of behavior and language even when we don't want to or it doesn't serve our best interest. The positive aspects of an automated reaction save us from having to rethink everything that happens to us in a given day. We just react to whatever is happening as we have so many times before. This can be lifesaving, as we quickly remove our hand that has touched a hot iron or stove, or don't step out into traffic when we see a car approaching. We don't have to decide, we just react.

The negative aspects include the very same thing. We just react. When we are not actively directing our thinking it just constantly goes on by itself. As many new meditators have found out when instructed to be still and have 'no thought,' the mind never stops thinking. So we can disassociate and become the observer, or we can choose to direct our thought anywhere we want by simply directing it, but we can't stop thinking when our conscious awareness is focused in the mental level of our being.

Being still is hard. We think it sounds great in our overly busy lives, but when we actually try to do it we find it almost impossible. Physically if we try to remain still, we very quickly find ourselves wanting to move. Within a very few minutes, what sounds wonderful and desirable becomes hard and requires considerable effort to maintain. Mentally the same thing happens. While it sounds like it would be wonderful not to have to remember and think of so many things all the time, as soon as we sit still and try not to think we experience what meditators often call 'monkey mind;' that is, the more we try not to think, the harder it becomes and we find ourselves getting agitated within because we are unable to be still

We can change what we are thinking, but not THAT we think. In a very real way being still is an exercise in making conscious choices. It's not really that being still is an option at any level of life. A hallmark of life is motion. Where there is no motion, there is death.

What happens when we are still? When we are still, we become much more aware of detail. Smaller details are often missed when busily scurrying about in our daily routines on automatic. When we are still these now come into focus and subtle details become clear. But there is still more to it. Interestingly, as we slow down physically and mentally, our awareness increases. What we give attention to expands, so when we are as still as we are able, we notice the smallest of details. Seeing life at that level not only brings a sense of awe at the intricacy, beauty, and order everywhere present, but paradoxically creates an awareness in us of the vastness of life. What in a linear sense feels like going to the small, holographically expands us in all directions, so our experience is that of seeing a larger world. The smallest and the largest.

You are Life itself living through you. You get to choose whatever experience you have by what you give your attention to, how deeply you pay attention to it, and what you decide it means (how you interpret it). It's not that one interpretation is right or true. Whichever you choose becomes its truth for you, and you experience life from that perspective. You can just as easily choose another perspective and you will then experience it entirely differently.

Mindfulness—being as fully conscious as you are able—is a necessary and often absent first step. The world would be vastly different if more were practicing this attention to mental activity. That said, once we have learned to pay attention to the present moment, we must then ask, mindful of what? What is it we are giving our attention to? What are we telling ourselves that it means?

Our mind never stops. Any beginning meditation student asked to empty their mind and think about nothing will tell you what a futile and frustrating experience that is. The harder you try, the more different paths the mind finds to wander down. Many just give up in frustration or find it yet another proof of how they are 'not good enough.' That misses the intended point of the teaching. Like many Eastern practices the point is to demonstrate in your own experience that it is impossible. That IS the point.

Once you realize the impossibility of curtailing the mind's constant automatic activity, you realize the importance of directing your thoughts intentionally. Left unattended, your mind will endlessly wander over the well-worn paths of previous experience and interpretation. This reinforces those perceptions as being real by one more repetition, and increases the likelihood of thinking of them as true reality.

So it's important to become mindful. But then we must ask ourselves, mindful of what? Once we have realized that constant activity of the mind, we understand the importance of directing it if we don't want just repetitions of old patterns to be our sole life experience. The question is then in front of us. To what do we direct our attention? To what we find most important? To what feels good? To things that intrigue us?

Inherent in each of us is the strong desire to belong and be significant. We ask questions like, Why am I here?, and What is my purpose? Initially, once we choose to direct our attention much of our effort goes into investigation. What is important and why? How large is our context of meaning and what is its source? Is it just about me, or my family, tribe, nation, race, or religion? All are important and the appropriate level of focus is different in different moments, but generally the smaller our frame of reference the less big picture our conclusions are likely to be. We realize if we want to belong, we need to ask ourselves what it is we want to belong to and why? If it's just myself I'm concerned with I can choose whatever feels good or attracts me.

However, as soon as we recognize our interconnection we then must take others into consideration. We then must weigh other's opinions, cultural expectations, the rules of the family, tribe, culture, and religion. While many may fit us, there will always be those that don't and we begin the dance of relationship. If we want to belong (fit in) and have a significant relationship in this group, then our choices are at least somewhat dictated by previous experience; our own, the group's, the collective. This is fine as long as they are congruent, but inevitably conflict begins here. As with everything there are both positives and negatives inherent. We wouldn't get much done if every person had to constantly rethink every little thing. Think of the millions of 'how to' questions we go through every day, yet each previously trod path we tread necessarily precludes other possible experiences. This is inevitable and it also underlines the importance of our choices. To the extent we mindlessly just repeat whatever we have been taught or done before we have the safety of knowing what to expect. Sometimes that is helpful and allows us to keep our attention on what is more important, but it can also lead to the boredom of nothing new here, as the price for the comfort of the familiar. The more fear-based we are in a given moment, the more likely the safe choices are to seem appealing. When the thrill of adventure or desire for something new are present, we choose differently. Something we haven't done before or outside the rules stipulated for fitting in and belonging presents itself and we have to make a choice.

There are other little recognized negative aspects to our mental function. While our intellect and reasoning powers have been rightly appreciated for their ability to compare and contrast in what we call critical thinking, our brain has no ability to distinguish true from false. It just repeats what was there before. It also has no ability to distinguish between our personal perception of what is happening and the external reality. This is the source of the well-known eyewitness issue in court cases. Although often given undue credence by juries, legal professionals have known for years that the accuracy rate of eye witnesses is very low and varies greatly when more than one witness is present. Additionally, each time an event is recalled it is altered by suggestion or inexpert questioning. This is then added to the memory, and the next time it is recalled it includes the new additions with absolutely no sense that it has been revised. Several decades ago, psychology found this out the hard way when multiple cases of child care facilities were accused of child molestation. Lives and families were harmed as children reported that they had been abused, not realizing that the counseling interview process was affecting what was being reported in what is now known as 'false memory syndrome.'

The mental dimension of our being is also the home of the ego. It is the part of us that perceives ourselves as separate from our environment and others. It is where, by itself, the ultimate conclusion is that we are 'not enough.' As mentioned earlier, this is not a pathological deficit as so often treated in psychology, it is merely an accurate experience that consciousness at the mental level is incomplete. It is only one half of the consciousness possible to the individual human, and is the invitation for us to go further; that we are more. The ego is not bad, it is merely ill equipped to be seated in the central seat of control. The mental masculine needs the sacred marriage of head and heart, masculine and feminine, electric and magnetic to attain full consciousness of ourselves as we fully are. It is only from the complete consciousness of both that we then understand ourselves as both unique individuals and part of the unified whole of all that is.

Our ability at any moment to interrupt the automatic function of thought and direct our thinking anywhere we desire is one of our mental strengths. The whole concept behind the mindfulness movement currently so popular, is that by consciously choosing where to place our attention and focusing our conscious awareness on a particular thing we take control of our mental consciousness and are able to direct it with our intention. Within the holistic health community and psychology, research into the power of intention is demonstrating amazing results that challenge much of our previous thinking relating to human ability. It is important to realize the caveat that what our brain can do is direct our thought. It does not have any power; that comes from our heart, and it is only the power of the intensity of feeling in our emotional heart that determines the effectiveness we are able to deliver. This is a good example of the necessity for head and heart to work together to be effective. Thought without power can accomplish nothing, and power without direction is dispersed randomly. When put together we can do amazing things. First we must learn to be mindful. Enlightenment is the first step. When we have that awareness we can then direct our mind through meditation or inner knowing to expand beyond mental to the power source of the heart. We will be saying much more about this in the coming Chapter on emotion.

Since mental consciousness is most familiar and where our consciousness resides most of the time, there are a number of other experiences in this realm that we can usefully be more aware of. Let's take a look at perceptions and beliefs, either/or thinking, archetypes and the collective field of consciousness, self-talk, choice, free will, attention and intention, and stress. Awareness in each of these aspects of mental consciousness presents us with the possibility of real choice and self-direction of our lives rather than the default repetition that is the only other option when we are unaware. Because they are all parts of being mindful, they are all important in maximizing our mental function. Mental concentration is the essential first stage of meditation, and a significant part of the second stage of contemplation. It is an essential aspect of our growth into knowing our true self. The third stage of meditation is the experience of union with the divine, and happens only in our heart. Divine grace does as it wills, but to do what we can to place ourselves in a receptive position the first two mental stages, concentration and contemplation are an excellent place to start.

Perception and beliefs:

Perceptions are the way we receive incoming energy signals. They are our autopilot. They form a kind of grid that both determines what gets through to our conscious awareness and shapes what we think it means. Perception and beliefs are closely intertwined because it is our beliefs about ourselves, others, and our world that provide the interpretation and decide the meaning of what our perceptual grid allows through. We all live in a soup of energy signals of many kinds. It would be overwhelming if we had to be aware of all that is present and intentionally choose each thing to focus on. Our perceptual grid does this for us on automatic by favoring what is familiar to us. In other words, information that aligns with and affirms what we have already determined to be true is given preferential treatment. This is also tied to the brain's pattern recognition function; it is easier to recognize a familiar pattern. From a both/and frame of reference, perceptions both facilitate daily life by streamlining incoming data, and tend to keep us locked in the status quo rather than being open to new experiences.

Beliefs are what we hold to be true. They include any religious beliefs we may hold, but certainly are not limited to them. Beliefs may be ones we've chosen consciously, or ones we just absorbed from our parents or culture as statements of what is true. They reflect what we know we believe and those subconscious statements of reality about who we understand our self to be, how we understand our place in the world, and unconscious contracts we made with ourselves at pivotal points in our lives. Sometimes our beliefs come from repeated instances reinforcing the same point. Others from a single moment that froze into our consciousness with permanent repercussions.

For example, a parental challenge like who do you think you are, repeated whenever a child challenges their authority may lead to a lack of confidence and belief that we are not as important as others, even though that probably wasn't what their parents intended. Cruel comments can wound so deeply that we seal parts of ourselves off. One craniosacral massage therapist I know calls these sealed off parts of our energy system, energy cysts. As I am assessing someone's energy field I experience these blocked areas as dense, often taffy consistency areas in the fluid layers of the Heart Field, or sometimes as holes in the integrity of the field where the grid of the structured layers is interrupted. Limiting beliefs create fences around the electromagnetic level of our Heart Field keeping us from full connection with divine Source.

Likewise positive beliefs such as, You can do anything you decide to and are willing to work for, empower us with self-confidence and encourage perseverance. Our words have power. They are our thoughts spoken into form. We most often are just aware of the expressive part of our statements. As we attain more understanding of their creative aspect we choose them with much more care.

This is true for all of us, but with added import in the case of small children. In the early years from one to five a child is just acclimating to the world and developing a sense of what kind of a world it is, who they are, and how they fit into it. It would be difficult to overstate how foundational the early beliefs they come to hold are in how they perceive themselves for life. Questions such as: Is the world a safe and friendly place? Am I loved? Am I valuable? Can I trust others? All are decided in this very brief time and impact our perceptions of all that happens from then onward through that lens. Life is dynamic and so these early beliefs are not unchangeable, but because our immature brains are incapable at this stage of rational thought, and we have very limited language development, these beliefs are stored symbolically very deep in our subconscious memory. They are not accessible by cognitive behavioral methods of talk therapy in my twenty five years of psychotherapy experience. Some cognitive recognition can occur, and thinking and behavior may be modified, but the deep emotional feelings are stored somatically and must be addressed at the level of vibration, frequency, and energy for complete healing. In the next Chapter on emotion (or energy in motion) we will discuss specific ways and modalities that show efficacy in restoring our energy coherence.

On a positive note, today's parents seem much more aware and persistent in working to instill positive self-regard in their children. To be effective energetically the reinforcement must be in alignment with the actual nature of the experience. Children at every age are quite energetically perceptive. It sends an incoherent and dissonant message when they are rewarded or praised for something that is not connected in reality with what is occurring. A child concludes that they cannot trust their feelings when a well-meaning but misguided adult praises or rewards behavior that has not required effort and focus on their part. Political correctness is a social imitation of acceptability or actual value that is not felt. It makes people angry because on the level of energy we feel a disconnection between what is actually felt and what is being said. A genuine accolade of admiration or appreciation that recognizes real effort and persistence and affirms one's sense of value reinforces it as desirable behavior. Note that it is not connected with whether it necessarily succeeded, but with the intention and effort put forth.

Either/or thinking:

Sometimes called 'all or nothing thinking,' 'black and white thinking,' or 'closed thinking,' either/or thinking denotes a very limited level of thinking that is binary, linear, and absolute. Choices are limited to this or that, right or wrong. Typical and normal in the stage of adolescence where the higher functioning parts of the brain have not yet matured, in adults this type of thinking represents a defensive posture. People who do not feel safe in the world or have a sense of trust from earlier emotional wounds have a guarded persona, and keep parts of themselves closed off, often from even their own awareness, as a safety mechanism. Sadder still, energetically operating from a closed system with emotional blockages precludes forward movement that depends upon an open exchange between self and others and our environment, and is often a sign of arrested development.

Either/or thinking forms the basis of the victim mentality. In a very real sense it is a slavery of the mind. Because it truly feels like threats are external, these folks spend an enormous amount of their time and energy trying to manipulate and control others and their environment. It feels necessary to do this to protect their own wellbeing. Since the only one we actually have any control over is our self, this never works out well. Yet we are unable to risk the challenges of something different or new if it feels like our safety is at risk. No amount of reasoning or explanation is sufficient, even if we agree with it.

Often persons locked in this type of thinking experience even further rejection and hostility from others who don't appreciate being manipulated or controlled. This confirms to them the need to maintain their defenses; a real catch 22. As you might guess, feelings of resentment, frustration, and anger are often present, adding layer upon layer of energetic dissonance that eventually leads to dis-ease.

The solution lies in the very needs that are not met. When the person is able to be in a setting where they feel safe, are able to trust the other, and are genuinely loved, healing can occur. The challenge is that those things must be true on the level of frequency and vibration, which is to say, genuine. The emotion or experience of energy flow must be in alignment with what is being said and done. When that happens, for instance when the person falls in love with another who returns the love, or in a constructive counseling setting, transformation can be rapid and healing complete.

Archetypes:

It was Freud a century ago who first identified consciousness explicitly, and noted that it had at least three different dimensions he called the id, ego, and super ego. These made up our personal consciousness. Later, his student Carl G. Jung went even further to say that there is also a collective unconscious in which we all take part. He coined the word archetypes to describe energy patterns existing in the collective unconscious which influence our thinking and behavior.

We have already said that our brain analyzes by looking for pattern recognition. Archetypes are energy patterns that are in the collective rather than personal unconscious. These patterns are not static, but are dynamic and constantly being altered as people are energetically connected to that particular archetype. The Myers-Briggs Personality Inventory, the Enneagram and other personality typing inventories are based on archetypes or patterns of behavior or thinking typically used by a person in a particular type of situation. There are many archetypes that have been identified, and perhaps more which have not. In popular culture, tarot and other card decks with archetypal qualities are used to facilitate helping a person recognize particular qualities that may be influencing them in ways they hadn't recognized. It's simply a way of looking at something from a different perspective, a change of observational viewpoint which can often help us see aspects of a situation in a new light or with more clarity.

There is nothing magical about archetypes. It does not require any particular skill or giftedness on the part of another to interpret them, although it can be helpful sometimes to have someone more knowledgeable about the qualities of specific archetypes explain the common qualities associated with that pattern if you are not familiar with them. Like the symbols that come to us in our dreams, archetypes don't have just one specific meaning and only you can verify how they show up in your life. They are patterns evolved through human repetition and stored in the collective unconscious or akashic record, so they have an influence on us even though they are not from our own personal experience. We all have access to all of them, but we find that certain ones are frequently present for us. Understanding the pattern allows us to apply it with more intention if it is useful to us, or change it if it gets in the way of our good. As we change it through our choices, it also alters the archetype in the collective. Like attracts like in the invisible realms, and so we align vibrationally with the frequencies or harmonics of the archetypes we are in tune with. On the level of the collective, they probably serve the same function as perception does individually; we each don't have to think everything through but can benefit or be limited from previous experiences with that type of situation.

Earlier we said that we are holograms of light energy in a toroidal flow pattern. In a hologram every fractal contains the information not just of that piece, but of the whole. That being so, it really doesn't matter which fractal you choose to look at. The information of whole is present in any and all of them. The practical implication of that is that you can access any part of you from any part of you. Divine efficiency in action. Archetypes are one pattern that you can become aware of, and from any one of them, connect to the whole of collective unity. As you do this, the whole of the collective unconscious becomes more conscious and aware of itself. The tipping point which we are now experiencing is when enough of humanity becomes personally aware of this and the collective unconscious, becomes the collective consciousness. This is the Noosphere or mental layer of Earth herself coming into being.

Beyond individual archetypes, some schools of thought have grouped archetypes by inner and outer focus and alignment with particular elements. This grouping and cross referencing of archetypes adds another level of patterns of patterns, as we identify not just individual, but groups of archetypes that provide us with further understanding of how we take in and act out our human experience. For example, at IAM Heart which teaches the Sufi tradition of Hazrat Inayat Khan, Susanna and Puran Bair have taken the characteristics of the four elements, Earth, water, fire, and air, and cross referenced them with the spiritual paths of master, prophet, and saint. That provides a matrix comprised of twelve archetypes they find a sufficient basis for understanding our own particular life path and purpose. They look at the four elemental energy building blocks of creation and correlate them with the external, internal, or combination spiritual focus that individuals tend to follow. This can be helpful in our mental grasp of our own particular group of qualities and how they contribute to our life purpose, and in seeing that all of the qualities and paths contribute different but equally needed parts of the whole. Inherent in grasping this is the recognition that there is not 'one right way' for doing things or for any particular spiritual path. Of equal value to the whole, their expression and practice is necessarily different and particular.

Self-Talk:

All of us talk to ourselves all of the time. Some even do it out loud. How aware are you of the conversation going on inside your mind? Like everything, self-talk can be either positive or negative and is neutral in itself, but from years as a therapist as well as my own personal experience it seems likely that most self-talk going on automatically through our default mechanism is negative and critical. When we are paying attention to it, we have the option of evaluating it, deleting the negative and replacing it intentionally with a positive statement of that which we choose to create in our reality. When we are not, it impacts us at the level of feeling and colors our experience without our even being aware of it. Some of the harsh messages we would never tolerate coming from another, yet in our own head go unnoticed altering both our mood and our decisions.

At the beginning of this Chapter thoughts were defined as subtle energy realities. As such they have impact both internally and externally in our environment. When we are living just in our mental ego consciousness we think of our self as a separate and self-contained individual. If that is our experienced reality it allows us to say that what we think is our business and doesn't affect anyone else. From this perspective thoughts are 'not real.' From the larger perspective of thoughts as energetic realities that originate in the invisible realms and manifest as measurable energy waves in our brain, we see them as a first step in manifesting more concrete reality. They seem to be astride the invisible and visible dimensions of our being. Not yet an overt behavior, but altering the electrical activity in our brains and present in our consciousness.

Within the profession of neurology and allopathic medicine in general, consciousness and brain activity are regarded as brain produced. Several recent books by neurologists who have suffered traumatic brain injuries such as stroke or massive brain infections rendering them comatose for weeks or months have refuted this claim from their personal experience, in spite of their professional training that would say otherwise. Jill Bolte Taylor, a neuro anatomist experienced herself having a stroke and then in months of recovery was able to mentally observe her experience in spite of physical limitations that did not allow her to communicate. Her powerful report of a soul knowing and wisdom always present even though her brain was originally nonfunctional, now lead her to say, we are responsible for the energy we bring into any space. Having experienced the non-locality of consciousness and other dimensions of reality, she is now aware of how our personal energy, our Heart Field, affects not only ourselves, but also others and the environment around us. Likewise, neurosurgeon Eben Alexander, had a massive brain infection that left him essentially brain dead for many days. Even though that was medically confirmed by scans and other neurological measurements, Alexander had conscious experiences during that time of heaven, our purpose here, and other observations he reported in his book.

Backing up the years of research on near-death experiences, almost universally people having this type of experience have a profound shift in their understanding of who we are and the power of our mind and spirit in creating reality. Any fear they may have had toward death vanishes, and they return with a sense of humility, gratitude, and love along with a much expanded sense of our power to alter the reality around us, and vastly altered sense of what is important in life.

Whether we are aware of it or not, every feeling and thought as well as behavior we choose alters the fields around us. The vibrational frequency of our heart beat resonates not only within us, but also all around us, and even non-locally when we direct it with our thoughts and intention. It appears that the harmonics of our heartbeat have effects both locally and outside of normal space/time constraints. I like an old Gregg Braden quote I've kept on my desk for years. It reminds me every time I see it that, "Every moment of every day, what you feel in your heart is a command in the Mind of God. The Mind of God interprets our feelings very, very literally." When we remember that it is our feelings that are our sensation of energy movement and frequency, not our thoughts, it explains the underlying reason behind the frustration of many who saw the movie, The Secret, about the Law of Attraction, and then didn't understand why mental thought alone didn't manifest the reality. Our feelings are our frequencies; the harmonic chord of our actual state of being, and that is the reality we broadcast with every heartbeat.

The more conscious we are of the self-talk at our mental level, the more intentional we are able to be about choosing to say to our self what we truly believe and the thoughts we choose to think.

Choice, free will, attention and intention:

People are fond of believing that every choice they make is a result of their free will. It takes some time in life to realize that all of our automated default choices are not choice at all, but merely repetition of old patterns and familiar behaviors. While it is true that everyone always has the potential of free will, or ability to choose whatever they desire, the vast majority of the time we are not using it. Most of the time we are just reacting on autopilot. Reaction doesn't take any thought at all, it's just there. It may or may not serve us well. Likewise, when our beliefs circumscribe what we believe is true or possible, we never look beyond them. We don't choose when we don't believe there is a choice. There is ALWAYS a choice. Learn to recognize that when there doesn't seem to be one, it is time to shift perspective or seek assistance.

I mention this because it is so prevalent and unrecognized. When we are not being mindful, we are not making choices or using our free will. This is the underlying reason for mindfulness practices and training. Autopilot works without thinking about it. We don't know what we don't know. Once our awareness is awakened we are able to be more present in the present moment. More of our attention is in the now.

When our full attention is on what is immediately before us, rather than wondering if this meeting is ever going to be over, and what are we going to have for dinner, and I have to remember to pick up the kids at soccer..., we bring more of our life energy into this moment rather than having it divided up and scattered between past, present, and future. Let's say we have 100 units of energy available in every moment. If 50 of them are engaged in worry over the disagreement we had with our spouse last night, and 30 are trying to figure out how to get everything done on time before the day ends, that only leaves 20 units available in the present moment for what is immediately before us. Philosophically it's not hard to see that the present moment is all we ever have; the only moment in which we can act. Yet if we haven't developed skills that focus our attention in the now, what we bring to the moment is just some small portion of the life energy available to us. Choosing how much of our life energy to bring to the moment is up to us.

While attention is being consciously responsible for what we are taking in, intention is being responsible for what we are energetically sending out. Directing our thoughts is like choosing a channel on the remote. Many channels are available, but you direct by which button you push which one will come into focus. Intention sends your life energy as thought to where you direct it. Feelings, which we will be discussing in the next Chapter are the frequencies we are broadcasting, and they don't just happen. We choose them by our mental interpretation of what is happening and what it means. What is often not understood is that we can choose to change our feelings if we want them to be other than what just shows up on auto. How empowering to know they can be under our direction and control if we choose them instead of just letting them happen or thinking that other people are responsible for them.

Stress:

Stress gets a lot of press but is not really very well understood by many. Usually when it's talked about it's in the context of how to make it go away. Stress never goes away. It is just life happening to us and all around us. It stops when we die, not before. Much of our stress is of the mental sort and that's what we want to discuss here. Everyone is familiar with distress, far fewer with eustress. Eustress is good stress. It is the things that challenge us and help us grow and move forward in life. We feel great when we've met a challenge and now know in our experience that we are more capable than we were, or are able to meet expectations we weren't sure if we could. Eustress is trying something new. It is exhilarating.

Distress on the other hand is something we all are familiar with. It is when life challenges us and we are unsure if we are equipped or have what we need to deal with it. Distress is related to our perception that something may be harmful to us in some way, whether or not it actually is in fact dangerous. Distress too arises from past, present, and future. When something has already happened and we are unhappy or dissatisfied with our handling of it, we ruminate about it over and over in our mind. If it is in the present moment it presents a challenge we are not sure we are going to be able to meet well. Distress about something which may or may not happen in the future is called worry or anxiety. We go over and over in our mind what may happen. It feels like we are working on it, but actually we are just spinning our wheels. No action is taken, and the anticipated event may not actually occur. Our body's stress response is still invoked and the effect is the same whether the actual threat is real or not.

From whichever source, the biochemical cascade resulting from stress is designed to help us fight or flee. It's often called the fight or flight response. It is evolutionarily designed for a physical response. In today's world more of our stressors are mental than physical. More recently stress has received growing attention from health care professionals over the past several decades, as its impact on health has begun to be appreciated. An additional category—freeze—has been added. All three reflect degrees of our sense of our ability to respond to stressful triggers, and relate to our perception of the situation. Fight is the most empowered response, indicating directly confronting the perceived stressor and actively trying to overcome it. Flight is still active, but is less powerful, choosing to try to escape from the stressor which we feel unable to overcome. Freeze indicates the highest stress level, when we feel overwhelmed and powerless; we just shut down.

The opposite of the stress response is the relaxation response. It is impossible for our body to be in both states at the same time. The relaxation response can be induced in a number of simple ways, offering us the ability to defuse our stress levels whenever they arise. Changing our thinking habits in terms of our self-talk, and intentional choice of feelings and thoughts with mindful attention on an ongoing basis to our mental activity offers a gradual shift to new habits that more accurately reflect who we really are, and eventually become our new default setting.

Let's look at some simple practices that contribute to our mental peace of mind and allow for this level of our Heart Field to be in harmonious energy coherence with our body and spirit.

1. Breath.
   Slow, deep, and complete breathing oxygenates our brain allowing it to function well. It also stimulates the parasympathetic nervous system, lowering our blood pressure, heart rate, and inducing the relaxation response.
2. Smile.
   The simple act of smiling, even if you don't feel like it, also induces the relaxation response and improves our mood state. You can't maintain the stress response while smiling.
3. Mindfulness.
   The first step in becoming empowered mentally, or enlightened (in lightened), is to concentrate our attention on our thoughts. When we focus our consciousness by paying attention to what we are thinking we become more present in the moment. What we pay attention to expands, and what we remove our conscious energy from diminishes. The only thing needed to extinguish unwanted thoughts is to stop giving them our attention and energy. Once we are consciously aware of our thoughts, we can choose to redirect or reframe them if they are not congruent with our integrity and values.
4. Positive self-talk.

Opposite of the negative self-talk often found playing on old tapes in default mode, when we are aware of it we can choose to delete the inaccurate and destructive messages and replace them with positive affirmations of who we truly are and the qualities we wish to embody. We can become our own cheerleader, loving and encouraging our self, being forgiving rather than judgmental when we make a mistake, and gentle with our rate of progress. The universal spiritual injunction to "Do unto others as you would have them do unto you," can be just as helpful if you say it in reverse, "Do to yourself what you would have others do unto you."

5. Develop a daily mental health hygiene practice.
    It doesn't need to take long. A few minutes each day will go a long way and immunize you over time to stressful reactions. Once this practice becomes a habit, it will automatically kick in when a stress presents itself. Best done in the same place (your space will become energetically conditioned), just sit quietly in stillness and silence. Breathe in divine light and feel it settling through your body, into each cell, and clear down to your feet. With your exhalation first let go of any stressors, pains, or issues you wish to release. Once they are gone and you feel light and well, you can exhale your love and positive intentions on your exhalations, adding their truth, beauty, and harmony to the environment around you. You can fill your own Heart Field with all the qualities you want to take with you throughout the day. Concentrate on what you wish to magnify in your life, then hold the intention to take it with you throughout your day in whatever situations you find yourself. Many people do this as a breath prayer that they can silently repeat to themselves during the day whenever it comes into your awareness. The benefits of this practice don't stop when your practice time is over, but continue on for some time as you go about your day. If you are able to do this for a few minutes in the morning and

again late in the day before retiring you create an ongoing energy balance that facilitates good health at all levels.

6. Use the SPA method.

Not original with me, I recently saw this useful acronym, SPA. It stands for Shift Perceptual Awareness, and is an easy way to remember to shift our mental gears to a more positive and constructive level that serves our best self in love.

As we develop our concentration and contemplation we are also becoming equipped for the next stage of our access to our Heart Field, expanding our consciousness beyond mindfulness to the intuitive level of heart.

7 EMOTIONAL FACTORS

"We are each a magnetic field vibrating around our own nucleus and we want to learn how to vibrate with the cosmos."
Stephanie South

If you read nothing else in this book, read this Chapter. It's that important.

Just as your head and brain are home to mental function, thought and intellect, your heart is home to your spiritual function, feeling, and intuition. Your brain is dualistic, left and right brain hemispheres operating in a comparative binary system of electrical signals. Your heart is one, magnetically unitive and intuitively grasping wholes. Its language is not words, it is feeling and emotion.

Feeling and emotion are NOT what you probably think they are. Learning that they are energy frequencies and your primary vibrational messengers is likely a surprise, and is fundamental to your ability to perceive your life energy and direct it consciously.

The emotional layer of our Heart Field is a fluid layer. It holds all the colors of the light in a constant dance of flow and movement. Non-structured, it is our symbolic messenger, the intermediary of our soul and mind. Its language is feeling, the perception of energy movement.

Emotion is the language of energy. It is E-motion, energy in motion. As we learn to pay attention to our feelings and emotions we are becoming conscious of the state of our energy being. Balanced or unbalanced, congested, disconnected, or flowing freely in a state of wellbeing. What we experience as feelings or physical sensations in our body and emotion together make up the symbolic feedback system of the state of coherence of our life energy. Feelings are our perception of our own state of energy integrity within and between the dimensions of our being. They are the messengers from our soul.

This is very different than how our culture has defined feelings and emotion. It is necessary to learn their vibrational function in order to properly understand and value their actual roles in our health and wellness. Feelings are our experience of energy. Culturally, feeling and emotion have been seen as side effects, as a peripheral weakness of our human being; something to be controlled and contained. Associated with the feminine, they have been particularly devalued and maligned for males, and tolerated as a sign of weakness in females. Arising spontaneously out of our subconscious, it seems all the more threatening because feelings just appear, complete with a whole host of somatic affects and often no conscious awareness of its coming. We are easily embarrassed by a sudden rush of sensation that leaves us feeling vulnerable and exposed. In a society uncomfortable with our bodies in many ways and largely out of touch with them, feelings seem more a problem than an ally. This common socio-cultural view discourages any real examination and understanding of our feelings. When they are discussed at all, it is from a perspective of how to manage and control them. Little wonder they are so confusing to us. When we learn what every marketer knows, that every decision is made emotionally then justified rationally, it makes it all the more important to be aware of them. When we learn what Roger Callahan realized decades ago, that all illness and disease have an emotional cause, paying attention to our feelings becomes an issue of health and wellness.

When we learn the true role of feelings and emotion, it is very clear that we need to pay close attention to them. They are our energy messengers, the guide to what is actually happening within the multiple layers of our Heart Field. They are always an accurate reflection of the state of our energy and of our wellbeing. Actually feeling our feelings and learning to decode their messages to us is an essential skill in heart mind consciousness, and is the first step in healing dis-ease at any level.

Love and Fear

All cultures and spiritual traditions associate the emotion of love as coming from the heart. Yet few things are less understood than love. In our culture love has been defined as a feeling appropriate to one of two categories; romantic or sexual, and parental. These are considered acceptable and desirable situations to experience love. Some consideration is given for a platonic type of love found in deep friendships, but most think of love as just one of our feelings. In trying to describe it we use terms like attracting, magnetic, overwhelming, compelling, and all pervasive bliss and ecstasy. Once we've exhausted all the superlatives we can think of, we universally state the obvious; there just aren't words that can adequately describe it. None of us ever forget falling in love. It instantly and totally changes everything in life. The beloved is always at the forefront of our thoughts. Our mood is expansive, light, elevated, and joyful. Nothing else matters and we want nothing more than to be with that one all of the time, to feel this way for all time. The sense of connection and union is so strong we would to anything to protect it. What appears to be external, an other, we know at the deepest level is part of us. In them we see the reflection of who we really are, and invest in the belief that it is that person, place, or thing that is its source. We experience it internally, but believe its source is external to us.

Our misunderstanding of what Love is lies at the base of our sense of separation. It is not a feeling at all, although all the feelings mentioned above describe some of the many sensations we experience when we are conscious of its presence. Love is the very substance of the universe out of which all is created. Love is all there is. In spiritual traditions they say that God is love; not that God has a lot of love, that God IS Love. Love is all powerful, all knowing, and always present.

Love can never be absent. It is who we are. However, to the extent we are unaware of its presence and when we are not conscious of it we feel fear. Fear is the sense of being separate, alone and disconnected, not belonging, in danger, insignificant, not of value. It is the experience of our false self. When we believe love to be an external reality, conditions then come into play. There are places we must go, things we must do or not do, rules to follow, all toward the end of being worthy of that external reality being bestowed upon us. We have to earn it or deserve it. Someone, or something else seems to own the option of Love's presence in our lives. Pleasing them then becomes our total focus. Defense against all which appears to threaten us becomes the common state of our daily lives.

Love is our essence, our True Self. Fear is the absence of love in our conscious awareness. To the extent that we are feeling love, we have no fear. That is what is behind the spiritual injunction to 'fear not.' To the extent we are unable to perceive love as our experienced reality, by definition some form of fear is the only option. Fear is based on a lie that isn't possible. All of our addictions are efforts to numb the pain of not feeling loved. Healing cannot take place at the mental level because that is not where the problem is. Healing takes place at the level of our heart as the obstacles and disconnections that prevent us from feeling what is always true—we are love—are removed. This is a process of inner realization that cannot be produced by drugs or changing our thinking and behavior. These things can offer some short term control, but real healing can only occur as the false self of mental ego is transformed by becoming conscious of the experience of our True Self always present at the center of our heart, and transmuting ego from master to servant.

Once we understand that we don't need to go somewhere, get something we don't have, learn something we don't know, we are freed to shift our focus of awareness from the externals to the internal. Inner awareness is not something common today in our culture. There is too much power and money to be made by keeping us in the mentality of victim. Once we understand that inside our self is the only place we can find the truth we have always been seeking, we grasp the necessity of developing the skill of inner knowing. Authentic spiritual teachers have always taught this lesson. Inner knowing is, in fact, the meaning of meditation. It is where we experience union with the Divine; that God and we are one. Our True Self. As Chunyi Lin a Qi Gong master accurately calls it, the universe within.

We said earlier that concentration and contemplation are the first two stages of meditation and begin in our mental mind. The third stage is actual meditation, or experienced union with the Divine. This realization is of the Holy (Whole) Spirit that resides always in our heart. It is this level of heart-knowing humanity is now evolving into. Words can describe, but only the feeling, the emotion (energy motion) of it documents it in our experienced reality. In that process of the experience, we are transmuted. Our identity changes. We know who we are. Our energy frequency is raised. We experience our self as our True Self: embodied divine reality. Love is the composition and connecting link that integrates body, mind, and spiritual dimensions of our being into one whole, holy, being.

If we were to make this statement from our false self, the ego, this would truly be grandiose. It would possess the self-referential quality of narcissism. Made from the True Self aware of its union with the Divine in the heart, it is a statement of fact always accompanied by a deep sense of humility, awe, and reverence. True Self is always aware that this truth it now experiences is the reality for all, whether or not it is recognized. Someone living out of their True Self will always treat others with the respect due this truth, whether or not the other is aware of it. Experiencing our divinity is not an experience of superiority, it is one of connection, compassion, interdependence, and service. Its goal with others is to help them realize that this is also their truth. To see it in them when they cannot see it yet themselves.

In the next Chapter we will delve more deeply into the spiritual aspects of this and the relationship between religion and spirituality. Here we want to focus on the role of emotion and feeling and discuss the means of becoming more aware of what is happening energetically. Hopefully it is beginning to become clear why mindfulness is necessary, but insufficient. To know our True Self we must be able to expand our consciousness another layer out. To be as conscious at the heart level as we have been at the mental level. The heart level includes physical and mental awareness, but also much more.

Before describing practices that develop this inner knowing, it is helpful to have a sense of the anatomy and physiology of the emotional heart. Our physical heart, beyond its recognized role as the pump that circulates our blood throughout our body, is also the great communicator. The harmonic frequencies of our every heartbeat resonate instantaneously throughout our physical body through vibration of the water found in inter and extra cellular tissues, carrying instructions that coordinate all of our bodily processes. These frequencies also pulse radially outside of our body throughout our Heart Field and connect us with others and the environment around us, and non-locally through quantum entanglement. The emotional heart is at the center of our physical body. Larger than our physical heart which it encompasses, our emotional heart extends from its depth at the base of our solar plexus to right above our throat, encompassing chakras three, four, and five.

Our arms and hands are extensions of our heart. As moveable sensors and emitters they receive and transmit energy frequencies to and from our heart. When we put our arms around someone, we bring them into our Heart Field where their Heart Field and ours synchronize energetically. This is bi-directional, with the highest and most coherent of the energy frequencies bringing the rest into coherence. If both are already coherent, it magnifies the signal strength and resonance capacity. This goes on whether or not we are aware of it. We are always communicating the frequencies of what we are feeling.

In research I designed and conducted a decade ago, The Heart Field Effect© demonstrated clearly the connection and synchronization of heartbeats between people when they were in the three to five foot space we think of as our 'personal space.' This occurred without touch of any sort. It was accompanied by significant positive shifts in experienced symptoms of distress of both physical and emotional nature. This healing effect happened without any touch, technique, or intention at all, just being in the presence of the therapist's grounded Heart Field while she focused her attention on them. A growing body of scientific research and literature recognizes that disruptions in mood and thought are driven by disturbances in the body's biofield patterns. The power of presence, it turns out, is not just a euphemism but rather an accurate description of our actual energy impact not just within ourselves but also others around us. Not yet generally well known, this adds a whole new dimension to the healing relationship, and makes it clear that the emotional heart of the therapist is far more important than whatever techniques or therapy they may be using.

It is also something that doesn't require a professional therapist. Any of us can do this with our own attention and positive regard. How much power it has is dependent on our own heart's development, and the intensity of our feeling, but we all can do it.

Heart Centered Meditation

We don't need to become quantum physicists to get the basics of how e-motion works. Some simple practices help us expand our consciousness. This expansion is both deeper and higher from a 3D perspective. In a 4D view it is larger in every direction, deeper, higher, wider, forward, and backward. We experience this expansion not only as larger within this dimension, but as awareness in multiple dimensions. Because our heart is the location where the dimensions of body, mind, and spirit intersect, it is where we must locate our consciousness to experience them fully. We can start very simply.

As with all meditation we start with breath as we described in the last Chapter. Sit upright with feet on the floor and arms and legs uncrossed. Close your two eyes used to view the outside world, and open your third eye located on your forehead between your external eyes. This eye is one and is for inner sight, or insight. At first you may see nothing at all, just blackness, but as your meditation proceeds you often begin to see colors and lines or shapes, some familiar, some more abstract. Inner knowing is beyond language, and so the colors and shapes are symbolic. Just notice them if they appear, and note what feeling accompanies them.

Begin by noticing your breath. You will immediately notice that it starts to change as you pay attention to it. Notice if your inhalation or exhalation is longer or shorter. After a moment of gratitude extended to your breath, begin to take gentle but full and complete breaths, making them as slow, even, and complete as you are able. Use your abdominal muscles to empty your lungs completely on the exhalation so that on the inhalation all the air in your lungs will be fresh. Spend several minutes just feeling the sensations of your breathing, and after a few minutes you will notice that your breathing has established a rhythm of even, gentle, deep, and complete breaths. When you notice the rhythm is established and continues without requiring your full attention, it is time to move deeper to the heart.

Begin by focusing on the physical heart muscle itself. You may notice a flow of subtle energy, a sensation so light you might even wonder if you are imagining it. Your focus of attention operates much like the central point of an energy vortex. This is especially true within your physical body and in all of your Heart Field. See if you can feel your heartbeat. You might hear it, sense it, or feel its beating. Sometimes you don't feel it at all at first. That's okay, over time and with practice and patience you will. You know it's beating, so just be patiently expecting you will feel it, and soon you will. If it is helpful to you, you can place a finger on one of your pulse points to feel it externally until your internal perception kicks in.

Creating a focus of attention is not just a brain or mental activity. It occurs on many levels of consciousness. Wherever you place your attention within your body, or anywhere in your Heart Field, there is an immediate flow of subtle energy to that area. This energizes the cells of your body, and the light of your energy body. Focus creates quantum field effects which create distinct flows of energy, geometry and harmonics within you and torsion spins outside of you.

When you focus your attention and add to it feelings of appreciation or gratitude it has a synchronizing effect upon your energy field and upon the rhythmic magnetic emissions of your physical heart. This combination of focus and coherent emotion can be used to generate high states we experience as bliss or ecstasy. This is an important catalyst for evolution. Even a few minutes spent each day on focused in your heart with gratitude synchronize your consciousness with the harmonics of evolving Earth herself. Not only do we feel blissful, we radiate those frequencies into the Noosphere itself, contributing to the emergence into humanity's full consciousness of new waves of harmonic energy unifying our experience of human being.

In this practice you focus your attention on the physical heart. As you focus your attention on it generate the feeling of appreciation or gratitude. It is not the thought of appreciation or gratitude, but rather the feeling. Thought will not activate the subtle energies needed to generate ecstasy—only feeling is capable of activating the energy vortices within you.

As you focus on the physical heart and generate the feeling of appreciation, or gratitude, a waveform of energy flows throughout the body, carried by the magnetic field of the heart, which emanates outward from the physical heart to encompass your entire body. As the flow of energy begins throughout the body, there is a spontaneous arising of first lightness and freedom, and then expanding further to ecstasy or bliss, felt at the level of every cell.

Play with this a bit. Sense what happens in your body as you focus on your heart and generate these feelings of appreciation and gratitude. Physically feel what seems to be happening at the cellular level as the millions of cells of your body receive this coherent energy of gratitude or appreciation. Once you have built the ability to do this whenever you wish, you can start directing this powerful energy with intention. You can expand it to fill not just your body, but your entire energy field. See it gushing out the top of the head and flowing down over and through your entire

Heart Field. In the next Chapter on spiritual factors we will take this further still, not just looking at generating positive feelings, but looking at how feeling all of our feelings allows us to grow the dimensions of our heart to its full capacity.

Your Heart Field looks very much like a luminous egg when viewed by a clairvoyant or one of the technology instruments like the Biofield Viewer or Electron Photon Imaging (EPI). The wide part of this luminous egg shape is up around the shoulders and the more narrow part is around the feet. There is a central line or axis that runs through the center of this field (the hara), and through the center of your physical body, through the top of the head and down through the perineum. This line is the central axis of the magnetic Heart Field that comprises the subtle energy body. This holographic field extends above the head and below the feet a few inches, to a several feet, or even yards. In certain energy states it expands much farther. By shifting your attention to this central axis and to the field surrounding your body, you allow the bliss to move out from the physical body into the field. This creates powerful harmonic patterns that bring you into resonance with the waveforms of accelerated evolution that are flowing throughout the galaxy. Do not underestimate the powers of this practice. Though very simple, it is profound and effective.

The reference point for consciousness is established not only by belief, but also by one's emotional harmonics transmitted with every beat of your heart. What you hold the frequency of you align with. It can't be any other way. Your feelings are the experience of frequency. They connect to a thought. A thought is an energetic thing. So whatever you are thinking, whatever belief you are holding aligns you with that energy archetype or pattern and creates its expression in your reality. This is always the reality, the only thing that varies is our awareness of it. The opportunity and goal is the same for all humanity, but our own effort is required to make it our reality. As Fritz Perls said, "We must lose our minds and come to our senses." As we do, our senses, our feelings guide us faithfully to the path of heart consciousness.

Our world is rapidly changing. What once was deemed to be myth will soon be seen as real and become self-evident. We are creator beings in the midst of creating our future and the future of generations yet to come. We hold within our hearts a key to the mystery of our being. The opening into this mystery is through our capacity to enter these higher states. Developing our ability to expand our consciousness to our heart mind, become as at home there as we are now in our mental mind, and direct its immense power with our attention and intention requires the devotion and commitment to a daily practice of meditation in our heart. It is the beginning. Know that when you enter your heart, you enter into communion with all the masters who have and do serve humanity. Know that when you enter your heart, you enter into communion with your True Self.

We have said that Love is the reality, the substance of all that is. Meditation on the heart and in the heart takes us to the inner knowing, the experience of this reality.

Asking a Better Question

Another way we can begin to listen to our feelings is to do what I call, asking the next question.

Many years ago as I was about to graduate from Virginia Wesleyan College, a philosophy professor who had been a major influence on me then, and ever since, asked me, when you were deciding to come here you said you had many questions. Did you get them answered? No, I replied. He smiled and said, ah but now you are asking better questions. That brief exchange made a powerful impact, and has stayed with me ever since. At the time it just clicked and something shifted. Everything shifted. With that brief observation, Dr Larry Hultgren awakened me to a different perspective. It suddenly dawned on me that getting the right answer—what I had always striven for—might not be as important as asking the right question.

At this point, many years later, even the words 'better' and 'right' grate, for I now hear them as judgmental and limiting in themselves. However, the main point, to ask a different question remains a powerful tool in my healing toolbox. What does asking a different question do? It shifts my perspective, and in so doing it allows me to see the issue at hand from a different viewpoint. This immediately opens a new vista on whatever it is I am contemplating, and often this simple shift provides a whole new way of seeing whatever the issue, and offers new possibilities for addressing it. Over the decades since Dr Hultgren first made this statement to me on my graduation day—a parting gift that itself encapsulated the highest value of all I had learned in those years— to see things differently. I have used it countless times since, with myself and with others who seek my counsel as they face perplexing life situations and issues.

Our immediate automatic reaction when faced with a question or choice is to seek the 'right' answer. We advance from reacting to responding, by asking a question instead. And the question is always the same—"What does love look like here?" This shifts us into our heart. This simple action immediately expands our consciousness from just the conditioned mental pattern repetition cycle to one that includes our conscious expansion into our heart. This allows us to shift our primary focus to our feelings first. As we do this, our feelings—or energy messengers—come into conscious focus. Then, instead of an instant search for an answer, our attention comes into the present moment and we become conscious of how the question or situation affects our energy flow and function.

As we acknowledge the feelings by asking the questions, what am I feeling, and what is it connected to, our present moment focus allows an expanded awareness of the whole to supersede the conditioned reflexes of our mental analysis and judgment. These mental reactions are based upon past conditioning and beliefs and do not bring us into the consciousness of present moment living that is advised by all religious and spiritual traditions. As we acknowledge our feelings, our energy flow is restored, our feelings are 'metabolized', and we experience the shift from the mental either/or thinking pattern alone to the inclusive and whole perspective of the heart. Here we can accept feelings as messengers, shifting the good and bad judgments of the past into a present moment focus on hearing the whole message. It also includes giving ourselves permission to recognize and experience (feel) both the positive and negative feelings as equally valuable. As messengers there is no judgment attached to them at all. Fully present in this one moment, we are free to feel all of what is present, and make the appropriate connections to provide us with the clearest possible picture of this unique moment. This allows us the broadest possible perspective to make an intentional choice that honors the uniqueness of this moment while bringing the lessons of past experience with opportunities for new options, creativity, and imagination. It informs the best choice we are able to make in the present situation and moment.

Both/and means I have these feelings: AND I have these (often contradictory) feelings. How do I embrace and honor both? How do I love the negative as well as positive? Then we can stop languaging the negative as 'whining' (which implies a 'shouldn't') to this is happening AND both feelings are real. Here in the heart it is easy to see that both kinds of feelings are important. What would it be like to celebrate both? To genuinely feel gratitude for the value of the messages they bring?

Instantly several changes occur:

1. First we recognize we're automatically 'stuck in the story.'

2. Then we can allow and name all the feelings present.

3. Gratitude—we can be truly grateful for them bringing us equally important messages about the situation.

4. Reframe—rename—the 'negative' from the judgmental good/bad of positive and negative, to the balance provided by seeing the whole.

5. Acknowledging both/and; seeing where they come from and what they are connected to.

6. Make a conscious choice that honors both.

Just like the 'dieting' advice I give persons wanting to lose weight—eat whatever you want, whenever you want, just do it consciously--this method

1. Trusts self (body and mind)

2. Gives permission to allow the use of both imagination and creativity to create anew; a growth option that encourages fresh thinking and choices, ultimately expanding our options.

3. It lets you 'hear' feeling messages consciously; i.e., you 'get the message.'

4. Both/and; your choices then can honor both, not just the positive, requiring you to ignore or submerge the negative.

The outcome of all of this is:

1. Choice from an expanded consciousness that is loving (honors all feelings as equally important)

2. Mentally looking for the 'and' of both/and instead of the lower and more limited 'either/or', we've been socialized to is how we mentally expand.

3. It brings coherence intentionally into our consciousness.

4. It thereby changes our physical, biological response in our internal chemistry. It lowers stress, inflammation, and dis-ease.

5. Spiritually, we are congruent (coherent) in coming from our whole selves; i.e., being our true self. Honoring self and other, inner/outer, part/whole equally; making choices that are balanced, and that balance us at all levels of our being. Instead of getting caught up in our stories—the automatic reaction (read unconscious—it just happens), we ask:

What am I feeling? What's that about? What would love look like here?

Notice how immediately your body thanks you; it relaxes. Your mind thanks you; it feels peaceful and calm. Your spirit thanks you –you are experiencing wholeness in the present moment.

Pain
A final thing we need to address within the emotional aspects of our Heart Field is the issue of pain. Whether physical or mental in origin, pain is a loud energy signal. It demands your attention. Other than a physical trauma that occurs suddenly and of course requires immediate attention, pain from other physical and mental sources usually begins in a minor way. It's only when we continue

to not pay attention to the message it brings that it becomes louder and louder, more painful, until we do. This is true for both physical and relational pain. Because the energy message is always related to our wellbeing and ignoring it allows something destructive to continue, the increase in pain intensity is actually a very loving gift, although that is not how we originally perceive it.

Until we learn that feelings are energy messages and attend to them as quickly and fully as possible, our usual reaction to pain is to try to make it stop. Mentally we do this by suppression or repression, submerging it in less aware levels of our consciousness, hoping it will just go away if we ignore it long enough. If it's physical in nature we often use drugs to mask the symptom without doing anything to find and address cause. When chronic pain is present we often develop addictions to numb us temporarily from it. From whatever the source, the longer we keep from giving our attention to the message of the pain, the more destructive it is in our lives.

Beyond our own personal experience with it, our interconnections with others also suffer. If we don't transform our pain we will always transmit it to others. Resonance entrainment of our energy goes on whether we know it or not. We are responsible for the energy we bring into each space of our lives. If we wish to be of service in the world, our first responsibility is to take care of ourselves. To the extent we don't, we not only suffer but we pass it on to others.

I would like to share with you the message of the lepers. In this day and age most of us have never seen a leper. Many would be challenged to even explain what leprosy is. You might wonder why I am even bringing it up since it is so rare. I do so because there is a powerful message for us in understanding this condition. Leprosy is a disease in which a person's pain receptors are destroyed. They literally don't feel pain. While our immediate reaction to that might be isn't that great, quickly in observing what happens over time we realize it is not.

Without the attention getting a perception of pain, a leper can touch a fire or hot iron and not realize they are getting burned. They can sustain a deep cut or get an infection and have no indication that anything is wrong. Over time they often lose fingers, toes, and limbs from things that could have been treated fairly easily, except they did not have pain to bring their attention to it. They do not die from the disease itself, they die early from destructive outcomes from things not felt. I share this story not to be gruesome, but to help us appreciate that pain too is a gift of Love, and in the hope that we will all learn to pay attention to it when we are first aware of its presence.

We spoke earlier about the power of feelings of gratitude and appreciation in creating higher frequency states. When we want to transform feelings of pain there are also useful tools we can use:

1. Feel the pain. This is counterintuitive, but the most important thing we can do for several reasons. The experience of feeling it consciously is like telling our body, I got the message. Once the message is delivered it has served its purpose and doesn't need to remain. Notice where in your body it is located and describe what sensations it produces.
2. Attend appropriately to any physical needs brought to your attention. The same holds true for mental or relational needs. Do what you can to address the cause of the pain.
3. When the pain involves relationship issues with others, examine what part of the situation belongs to you and make whatever choices and take whatever actions you can to accurately reflect your true sense of what is loving to yourself and the other.
4. You have no control over others. The only one any of us can change is our self. Whatever parts of the issue belong

to others you can share your thoughts and feelings with, but what they do or don't do is up to them. This is where letting go and forgiveness are needed. After taking whatever steps you can, letting go of the outcome frees you from being stuck in something you have no control over, and keeps it from harming you further. Do what you can, then let go of the rest.

5. Forgiveness is another very misunderstood process. Forgiveness is NOT about saying something wasn't wrong or hurtful. It's not saying it was okay or doesn't matter. It's not about letting the perpetrator off the hook for their actions. Your forgiveness is actually for yourself. It frees you from carrying the hurt with you and removes you from the other's control over you with whatever the issue is. It clears your Heart Field of the muck created by holding onto negative energies. It takes away their power over you and restores your own energy integrity. They may have traumatized you in some way, but you get to choose how long you will carry it and allow it to affect your life. Forgiveness is the gift of freedom to yourself.

I began this Chapter by saying it was of the utmost importance to understand what feelings and emotion are. In life energy terms they are indicators of the integrity and free flowing nature of the different parts of our Heart Field. This elevates them significantly on our list of personal priorities from how our culture sees them. Positive feelings indicate clear flow and good connection. Negative ones indicate obstructions or disconnections. Both are equally important. They are our feedback system from our Heart Field. When we don't give them the attention they deserve, we are like the leper, likely to suffer the consequences of our not receiving the message they have brought us. When we do attend to them quickly and regularly we enhance our life, health, freedom, growth, and capacity for joy.

8 SPIRITUAL ASPECTS

For thousands of years now, a little over five thousand to be more precise, humanity has focused on the external and transcendent aspects of God. Religions have been the main venue for spiritual life, and the masculine principle predominated. God was anthropomorphized in multiple ways, the wise old man in the sky probably the most familiar to us. The Divine is of course transcendent. There is nothing that God is not. We have said that God is Love, the very substance out of which all is created. Yet we all have a very limited understanding of what that means. What more are beginning to realize is that transcendence is just one half the story.

That message was brought to humanity explicitly at the beginning of the last age, as Jesus of Nazareth modeled and taught the immanence of God. Five hundred years after Buddha gained mental clarity and became enlightened, sharing that process with his followers, Jesus came with the next step, to teach and model the religion of Love and presence of the divine in each of our hearts. He said it explicitly, "I and the Father are One. I am in Him and He is in me." This is what we mean when we say, Christ Consciousness. It is not something only meant for Christians, but rather a statement true for everyone when they consciously realize the ever present divine within. It does not mean that everyone has to worship or believe in that person, it means they need to get the message and experience it within themselves. We've worshipped the messenger and missed the message.

Early on, leaders within the Christian religion struggled to explain this paradox. Most notably, in 324 AD, the Council of Nicea debated whether Jesus was fully human or fully divine. They settled it theologically by saying he was <u>both</u> fully human <u>and</u> fully divine. This became one of the basic creeds of the Christian church. It of course makes no sense logically to our either/or brain. To be fully something excludes anything else in the language of reason. What Jesus realized was the presence of God within himself; experienced not in mind but within his heart. In Christian theology this is the Holy Spirit in the Trinitarian concept of God. Jesus also saw and taught that this was the inherent truth for everyone, although his followers largely missed this part. Instead they placed the messenger on a pedestal, worshipping him as a perfect being and denigrating themselves and all the rest of humanity as unworthy crumbs under the table. This placed us all in a victim status, inherently flawed and in need of an outside rescuer, a savior, to come and rescue us. It also allows us to avoid our responsibility for what Jesus taught, "All that I do you can do, and more." Our avoidance doesn't change the reality. As fully human, he modeled for us what is possible for all of humanity; more than possible it is our destiny.

Over time patriarchal control unbalanced by much more than lip service to females and the divine feminine principle became dominant both in Christianity and equally so in most of the world's religions. All persons have both masculine and feminine energies present at the level of their True Self. At the spiritual level there is never any conflict within the sacred marriage of masculine and feminine. They are both essential aspects of the whole. It is what holy means. It is only in our human immaturity that this becomes adversarial. The less a person is aware of this reality the more likely it is that they will feel threatened by the opposite gender either internally or externally. When women do not have an equal seat at the table of power in religion this natural balance is missing, and destructive outcomes are inevitable. Obvious to the most casual observer, men are in all the top positions of power and women make up the largest majority of attendees and work force in most religious groups today. Because our religious beliefs form our value system, this bleeds over into the cultural choices and rules we make as well.

The famous psychologist Carl Jung noted that what he termed individuation, or whole being, occurred around the age of sixty for those who continued the growth of their consciousness throughout life. As he observed human growth and development he found that the individuation process occurred in both males and females, but in opposite order. Males upon reaching adulthood focused on their own individual development first. Personal focus remained internal until middle age when the famous mid-life crisis begins the shift in perspective to an external focus on concern for others, a nurturing, mentoring, other oriented approach. Females, perhaps as part of our life bearing role focused first on the external, on others, nurturing, care giving, groups, and so on during their early adulthood, and then at mid-life started to shift to a more internal focus on their own personal growth and development of their talents. Somewhere around age sixty a balance between the two becomes a reality for those who remain growth oriented, and then both males and females can call on whichever qualities are best suited in the moment.

This was certainly the pre-shift pattern, although there are substantial signs that this is rapidly changing. A more androgynous sense of being seems to be much more common at younger ages now, with the millennials taking for granted as natural what once took much more growth and maturity to process. Both the masculine and feminine qualities seem to be much more consciously present to them. Perhaps this is one aspect of the collective unconscious becoming more and more conscious every day.

Religions have also provided many positive effects. All religions have provided the constant reminder to humanity that we are a part of a much larger story. The rituals that are an integral part of every religion remind us, orient us, and return us to this larger context of life. They have given us a context of meaning. While science asks how, religion asks why. Religions have provided a community in which to share the experience of Spirit, and passed on the teachings of the great spiritual masters throughout the years. Religious rituals can provide the experience of the transcendent and connect the important passages of our life with spiritual reality. Social support and group belonging are important aspect of religious community and are offered to anyone who chooses to join in.

In spite of all of that, religion in the United States has been in steady decline for the last half century. Whenever anything is out of balance on an ongoing basis, disease occurs. During this same time, religious extremism has increased. Several decades ago a new category had to be created by pollsters, and demonstrates consistently that while religious affiliation continues to drop, the rate of people identifying themselves as 'spiritual but not religious' has been growing at a rapid rate. What is this about? It's actually a very positive sign.

With its primary focus on transcendence, religion tended to separate instead of unifying. The transcendent is about the external, the world out there. Our lived experience is always about the world in here—our inner experience. So when only half the story is focused on, our vision becomes skewed. While the transcendent creates in us a sense of awe at the vastness beyond our ability to comprehend of this amazing Love, without the equal emphasis of its constant presence within, it makes us feel small and inadequate. What is unconditional love feels conditional upon right beliefs and behavior; something which needs to be earned.

What originated in an earlier worldview which saw and experienced everything in life as part of the whole, over time came to be associated with teachings of a particular person. The emphasis shifted from the message to the messenger. Loyalty to that person and their particular way of stating and practicing spiritual reality replaced the underlying commonality of the message. The universal message that there is only ONE became fractured into whose god is the real one. Once the association shifted from the oneness to the particular teacher, the external representative, what essentially unifies us became more and more the cause of separation. Persons dedicated to Spirit removed themselves from ordinary life and lived in cloistered places where the sole focus was on that particular spiritual path. They were 'called apart' to 'be in the world but not of the world.' Separated from the daily hustle and bustle of life in the world this visibly and practically reinforced the spiritual as something separate.

Then as human knowledge and mental development continued, science came into being separating worldly knowledge from spiritual and seeking to examine and define the world of matter objectively. Note the word object-ively. External reality was perceived as objects, the internal world as subject. Again we separated, now external from internal. Subjectivity was understood as our unique individual experience, not connected to the outer world of form, and therefore irrelevant. The visible and invisible worlds were regarded as different things. Matter and energy were understood as inherently different and therefore obeyed different laws. As some early scientific discoveries conflicted with the teachings of religion, additional separation was added as an agreement that science and religion were separate paradigms and would not impinge upon each other. This seemed to work for a while; the discrepancies were deemed irrelevant because the two worlds were not connected. In the world of science, the invisible became not real. In religious life the world was seen either as illusory or a distraction from what was really important, the invisible world of spirit. In both the connections and relationships of the whole were lost.

This is not to say that truth was ever lost. It has always been present for those 'with eyes to see.' They are the mystics among us, the seekers unwilling to accept the cultural story when it conflicted with personal experience. Although persecuted in ways varying from being killed to socially ostracized and ridiculed they continued to define for the rest of us the larger truth. For many hundreds of years their witness and teachings went underground to survive. The mystery schools created elaborate means to maintain and pass on these truths within a world hostile to their messages. Lineages flowed from a particular teacher and were passed on in degrees of initiation to those who had proven themselves dedicated and worthy. For true seekers there was always a path of connection.

Art too has always been a way of sharing wisdom that slipped through the cracks of rational scrutiny undetected. Paintings, poetry, music, and writing convey the beauty and harmony of the truth beyond words. Symbols serve as a signpost to deeper and higher meaning, the resonance of both palpable to those open to the experiences of feeling.

In individual growth and development a sign of maturity is the shift from external motivation to internal motivation. For humanity as a whole there also comes the shift from external to internal. In observing life from the smallest to largest levels we see that cycles of expansion and contraction define the forward movement of living. As we reach the apex of one there is a turning, a complete change of direction needed to experience the other half of the cycle of wholeness. A transformation completely changes us in preparation for the new. Religions explored the outer, transcendental nature of the Divine. With the shift of the Galactic Convergence, we have turned the corner of the great cycle of descent and return. Spirituality, the inner presence of the Divine is making itself felt as a deep urge for realization of our True Self.

This is happening within everyone, although its conscious recognition varies greatly within the individual. Collectively there has also been a shift. The days of individual lineages have ended along with the need for secrecy. Interestingly this was confirmed over the twenty five years leading up to 2012, by the prophets of each of the world's great traditions announcing that the time had come to share their wisdom with all.

The season of division and separation has reached its zenith. We can now observe that the genuine benefits it brought are now outweighed by the fragmentation of life at every level. As Arthur Young's Theory of Process states, the greater the degree of specificity, the less degrees of freedom. The isolation of the particular, no matter how intricate, removes our awareness of its connections and relationship to the rest of life. We now suffer from an overwhelming and constant deluge of information and data without connection to any useful context that gives it meaning. We have a deep longing for a return to wholeness, authenticity, and integrity. From living and making choices based on other peoples' opinions and other people rules, to inner self-confidence and trust that you are the expert on you. It is time for all the disparate threads to become woven into whole cloth so we can finally see the beauty of the tapestry.

It first shows up in us as an awareness that the old no longer serves or works for us anymore. The dissatisfaction with what is, is typically followed by a season of confusion. We don't yet know what is next, but we have to let go of the old in order to make room for the new, without any sense of clarity of what is to come. We get pushed out of the comfortable nest, or off the edge of the cliff without any knowledge of whether we can fly.

There is no other. There is only One. Beginning to grasp the reality of that conceptually through the very science that took us away from it, doesn't prepare us for the implications it brings.

That takes longer to sink in. Quantum mechanics and physics have demonstrated that there is no separate thing called matter. All is energy, able to change form, but not its existence. The same rules apply at all levels. There is not one set of rules (Newtonian physics) for matter and another set (Quantum mechanics) for energy. That has been an accepted reality in physics for several decades now. What is more recent is our awareness that we humans too are an integral part of this reality; not separate observers, but participatory observers. This has been the essence of spiritual teaching throughout the ages. Spiritually we call it the Perennial Philosophy, "As above, so below. As within, so without." What science is now adding to that is a degree of clarity of what that looks like at the level of energy and vibration.

From the smallest level of the particle collider to the largest where our satellite cameras now reveal billions of stars, galaxies, and universes, we receive confirmation of a much larger story than we have ever known before. From the Earth centric views of the past we leap to a vision of our location within a vast network where we are just becoming conscious of our role and purpose. It is a whole new perspective in which what we think, feel, and do matters more than we previously suspected.

With one foot in a world of every kind of separation and the other stepping tentatively toward a world of unity, our sense of balance is upended. As our understanding of the world's story shifts, we find that we can't just add on another layer to what we already know. We have to let go of all that we thought we knew and with an open mind and heart leap into the dark; into the feminine, magnetic field of infinite possibilities. Into the greater Heart Field of the Living Matrix of which our Heart Field is a vital part.

This can't be done from the false self of the egoic separate self we know with our mental mind. From that vantage point it feels like annihilation. This work can only be done from within our heart consciousness. It is only within the heart that anything truly real can be known, as de Chardin told us. It's where the false self of our mental ego becomes transformed into our True Self.

In a recent newsletter the Franciscan writer Richard Rohr in speaking of True Self said,

> As (Thomas) Merton says, our point of nothingness is "the pure glory of God in us." If we look at the great religious traditions, we see they all use similar words to point in the same direction. The Franciscan word is "poverty." The Carmelite word is *nada* or "nothingness." The Buddhists speak of "emptiness." Jesus speaks of being "poor in spirit" in his very first beatitude. The Bible as a whole prefers to talk in images, and the desert is a foundational one. The desert is where we are voluntarily under-stimulated-- no feedback, no new data. Jesus says to go into the closet or the "inner room." That's where we stop living out of other people's response to us. We can then say, I am not who you think I am. Nor am I who you need me to be. I'm not even who I need myself to be. I must be "nothing" in order to be open to all of reality and new reality. Merton's reservoir of solitude and contemplation allowed him to see the gate of heaven everywhere, even on a common street corner. ...A Zen master would call the True Self "the face we had before we were born." Paul would call it who you are "in Christ, hidden in God" (Colossians 3:3). It is who you are before having done anything right or anything wrong, who you are before having *thought* about who you are. Thinking creates the false self, the ego self, the

insecure self. The God-given contemplative
mind, on the other hand, recognizes the God
Self, the Christ Self, the True Self of
abundance and deep inner security. We start
with mere seeing; we end up with
recognizing.

This is the realm of the heart. We spoke earlier about the
masculine and feminine principles of energy, and the masculine
nature of our electrical, active, intellectual brain function. The
feminine principle is embodied in the heart. It is magnetic,
receptive, and intuitive. The mental age of evolutionary human
development just completed was all about the brain and our mental
consciousness. The new age we have now entered is the feminine
age of the heart. The wheel has turned, and the descent of
transcendent down to meet us—God with us—is now beginning
the ascent of union; the immanent embodiment of the Divine
within, as us. It requires a new level of consciousness that we have
not known before. This is the nature of spiritual but not religious.
It is not about a special day, place, or type of activity set apart from
our daily life. It is about being in every moment of our day, living
from a different level of consciousness and awareness. It is about
growing into the full knowledge and power of who we are so we
can be responsible co-creators of manifesting the reality of heaven
on Earth.

When we talk about accessing the Heart Field at the spiritual level
we are talking about all that we are, integrated into whole being as
an integral part of all being. Our personal Heart Field is a
holographic fractal of the cosmic Heart Field. In a hologram every
fractal contains not a piece or part of the whole, but all of the
whole is present in every fractal. This is too much to wrap our
brains around, and can only be known in the experience of it.
When it occurs we are forever changed. Who we know our self to
be is different than before. It cannot be conceptually grasped with
our mental intellect, only known as experienced feeling within our
hearts. Recalling that our feelings are our sensory experience of
energy frequency, our vibration, our frequency raises to a new
octave where we see and experience everything differently.

As we align with a new understanding of ourselves as energy beings, as Heart Fields entangled within the larger Heart Field, our spiritual needs and understanding shift from a focus on the external to an inward journey toward an experience of union with the Divine. This is the third stage of meditation. As we become conscious of this interconnection and relationship we realize that our every feeling, thought, word, and deed affects the whole. We recognize and take responsibility for our place as co-creators. We shift our attention from trying to change 'out there' to changing anything within our self that is out of alignment with the truth of who we really are. We find we are not only children of God, but called into maturing into the full stature of a particularized expression of the whole of God. As our spiritual heart develops it might seem that our individual nature might shrink as our unitive sense grows, however, the opposite occurs. As our sense of indivisible union with God enlarges, so does our unique particularity. We realize our divinity in becoming most fully human.

How do we do this?

Meditation, or inner knowing, is what allows us to perceive the Divine grace that has always been present. As we deepen the stages of our meditation from concentration, to contemplation, we come to a space where our heart begins to breathe us. This is not a state of our doing, but an inflow of divine knowing that just appears within our awareness. There are not words that can describe this adequately, but we can say some things about it and how to make ourselves available to it. Ultimately, it is not something we do, it is grace bestowed. We can't make it happen, but it does require effort on our part.

Consistency is far more important than any particular length of time. You quickly realize this as you notice that when you are in meditation you lose track of time. It's more accurate to say that deep heart centered meditation occurs outside of space/time as we currently know it. Meditation is not some difficult skill you have to learn, it is a gift of stillness and silence you give to yourself. For those minutes you can let go of everything external, the to do list, work, kids, spouse, house, and whatever else demands your life energy during your normal day. You can "close your eyes and just go inside, and hear Spirit softly say, there is only Love, there is only Love. Love that heals, love that sets me free, there is only, only love." as one of my favorite Karen Drucker songs gently croons.

As you settle in to feeling your breath and your heartbeat, your awareness expands beyond thought to the sensation of feeling. Rather than detaching from feeling which takes our conscious awareness out of our body, in Heart Centered Meditation we dive right into our feelings, feeling them as fully as possible, and hold them in gratitude for the vibrational message they bring us. As we go more deeply into our feelings we discover that they are not 'good' or 'bad' they are just feeling, sensing the state of our life energy and bringing to our awareness areas needing our attention in some way. We don't replace one feeling with another substituting a positive for a negative as we did in the emotional level as a means to raising our vibration. At the deeper and higher level of the spiritual heart, it is clear to us that nothing can really threaten or harm us in any ultimate way, and so we are free to feel all feelings without fear. At the spiritual level there is only Love. And all that is brought into the experience of Love is transformed by the experience. In the full experience of feeling it is metabolized by our heart. Once we have received its message, there is no further reason for it to remain and the feeling just dissolves. Like a need that is met is no longer a need, a feeling that is felt is no longer that feeling.

We can also take a particular question or intention into our heart meditation if we have something we want to focus on or get an answer to. In the mental age just ended, there were many highly specific patterns of breathing and mantras or ancient names of divine qualities used to assist meditation in a particular way. Those are no longer needed since the energies available to us have changed significantly, although it is fine to continue to use them if they bring you joy. A simple meditation with your full attention on being present in your heart is sufficient now. When you make yourself present in this way, physically, mentally, emotionally focused on your heart, anything else needed will be brought to your awareness. As you honor your heart's guidance by responding in your thoughts and actions, you will begin to notice more and more synchronicities appearing throughout your day. Gradually your meditative experience extends into your daily life as your vibrational capacity expands along with your Heart Field to a new and higher normal, and the Divine orchestration of life at all levels begins to reveal itself to you. Ultimately we will find ourselves able to be fully present in each moment as our True Self.

A note of caution is in order for readers who may be new to meditation and subtle energies. There is often an expectation that something dramatic will occur if you are 'doing it right.' While occasionally that does happen, it is far more common that we don't feel anything. There is a reason we call them subtle energies. Sometimes we get a sensation so lightly that we think we feel something, but are not sure if we are just imagining it. This is a common perception. Usually the changes occur so subtly that we aren't even aware we've changed, and then one day you find yourself in a situation that would previously have caused you distress, and realize that you feel calm and centered and peaceful.

It's helpful to think of meditation as you would if an MD prescribed a medication for you. You wouldn't expect to take one dose and then be fine. You know that you will have to take a dose the prescribed number of times every day for some time to see any results. I hesitate to use that analogy, but recognize that it is likely to be a familiar one for many readers. All that is required of you is willingness coupled with the action of sitting in stillness and silence with a focus on your heart and an attitude of open gratitude and genuine expectation. If you do this for just ten minutes twice a day, in just a few weeks you will find your life transformed in significant ways. Within several months you will find that you would not give up your meditation time for anything, because of the overall effect it has in your life at every level and in every area of living.

Some people find sitting still almost impossible for them and the effort stressful, although both silence and stillness are so unusual to us that the initial impulse for most everyone is to want to fill in the silence and 'do something.' We have been conditioned to think that doing nothing is lazy and bad. Our mind usually protests at first as well, thinking thoughts like, this is stupid, nothing is happening, I'm wasting my time. However if you are one of the kinesthetic among us, a moving meditation may be more helpful. It can be a structured movement like T'ai Chi , Qi Gong, or Yoga, or more free flowing like walking in nature, or just standing with your eyes closed and your feet about shoulder width apart and just swinging your arms and upper torso from side to side rhythmically. If you are not sure what camp you fall into, play with it a bit. Try out several ways and see which ones feel best to you. There is no 'one right way' to meditate, it is a state of being that we enter into for the purpose of becoming as inwardly aware and conscious as we have trained ourselves to be in the external world. For most, a practice that can be done with eyes closed is very helpful at least at first. It's hard to develop an inward focus when we are looking at the outside world. Although initially this is a shift from one to the other, as we develop our inner knowing, we eventually get to a place where we can be equally present in both at once.

At the spiritual level of heart meditation we also have additional options for surrender and forgiveness. Within Spirit we no longer surrender things that create energy blockages for us, it is more a total surrender of all of who we are in service to the Divine. Forgiveness is no longer just for our personal issues, but more in alignment with Ho'oponopono, the Hawaiian communal practice in which recognizing our union with all others, we take on the responsibility for their wrongdoing as our own, and seek Divine forgiveness for us as part of them. We can do this for anyone once we have reached the unitive experience, and often long time meditators will find old ancestral traumas emerging for them to heal once they have cleared their own personal traumas and issues.

Meditation is the one essential spiritual practice. It is the inner experiential key for which there is no substitute. Until we experience our True Self, all spiritual practices get co-opted by our ego. While we may reach some significant stages of spiritual realization, the false self interprets them in an ego centric way that increases rather than decreases our sense of separation from others. This shows up as feelings of spiritual superiority, specialness, having gifts that others do not and similar kinds of attitudes. This happens a lot at the early stages of authentic spiritual development, where some level of spiritual connection and skill is known, but where the person still requires outside validation to feel valued and significant. This is a dangerous period. Once our ego gets hooked in this way our false self expands, and especially if it is fed by public recognition, it can keep us from further spiritual progress for quite some time. Heart Centered Meditation keeps us grounded in both spirit and in our humanity. It allows us to resonate with others and see their greatness even if they cannot yet see it in themselves. In reflecting it back to them we serve as mirrors for their remembrance and facilitate the emergence of their True Self as well.

There are many additional things that provide access to our Heart Field spiritually. Some are quite simple. Anything in which we are aware of beauty, harmony, truth, peace, and love is in alignment with Spirit and reminds us of its presence.

Nature showcases an abundance of examples constantly available when we have eyes to see. None of us can fail to recognize the grandeur of a sunrise or sunset, or smell the sweetness of the damp Earth after a rain. But there are too many examples to count everywhere we look within mother Earth's bounty; a dew drop on the flower petal, the unfolding of a fern as we walk in the woods, the soft rhythm of the waves or waterfall splashing gleefully over the rocks. The field of grain waving as one in the breeze of the morning. A procession of ants marching in perfect alignment as they go about their work. A tiny flower growing up between the cracks in the pavement. We just need to notice.

Then there are those same qualities we see in others. The smile of delight on a child's face as he discovers he can do something new. The look of satisfaction on a farmer's dirt-stained and sweaty face as he surveys the field he just planted. An artist totally immersed in their paint pots as they bring their unseen painting into reality on their canvas. The transporting harmony of a symphony played by many musicians, their parts united as one expression of melody and tone. A mother nursing her baby as she rocks her, both gazing into each other's face.

Group participation in rituals of all kinds attune us to the harmony of our unity. As we develop our inner spiritual awareness we also become attuned to the presence of other light beings, and we discover that they too are our family; another part of the One. I suspect there is no end to our spiritual growth opportunities as our hearts open in joy to the possibilities.

PART III

HEART CENTERED WELLNESS: WEAVING IT ALL TOGETHER

The Heart Field

9 HEART CENTERED WELLNESS: THE OVERVIEW

"Resonance is nature's way of transferring information."
-Edgar Mitchell

"I have been a seeker and I still am, but I stopped asking the books and the stars. I started listening to the teaching of my soul."
-Rumi

I didn't set out to create a new model of wellness. Coming out of a very Christian background I knew that a spiritual foundation addressed the essence of who we are and couldn't be left out of any life plan or activity. Although I had my share of concerns about how in practice Christianity and other religions equally seemed out of sync with their core teachings, especially how any of them could start with the affirmation that there is only One, and then fail to realize that by that very definition they were just various understandings of the same One. If there is only One, there can be no 'other.' This core failure of human recognition sits at the very origin of our sense of separation, and the many resulting separations we have created from it.

One of the key statements made by Jesus was, "I came that you might have life, and have it abundantly." I have always believed that, although the fractured and fragmented world I saw in every direction gave little evidence of its reality, it is what is meant for the world to be, for life to be, for all of us to experience. My life's passion has been in to find out what that means, what it looks like, how it works, and how to live within that reality.

A second teaching of Jesus seemed to point to much more for us than we have yet realized. "All that I do you can do, and more."

At a deep level I have always known that both are true statements. Not of some idealistic fantasy, but of the very real intention and possibility for our human being here on Earth.

When we look around us today, almost everything seems to contradict that possibility in a million examples and some very stark terms. It's clear we have largely failed to get the message. Yet in moments of crisis time after time we see people immediately and without thought, just rush to help each other, even at the risk of their own life. The goodness and compassion of people surges forth to neutralize and transform fear and evil. Both examples are present.

In both personal and professional life it has always felt necessary to bring all of who we are to the situations and settings we find ourselves in. For me, the desire to be of service to others, first led me to a career as an RN. I found myself drawn to those areas where the need was greatest, and married at the very young age of twenty one to my childhood sweetheart when he joined the Navy, spent more than twenty years working in critical care units of hospitals all over the country. There is nothing like an Emergency Department, an ICU, or an operating room to bring you face to face with life and death issues on a daily basis. Both the fragility of life and the strength of human will and compassion were brought home to me time and time again. There is an intimacy present in those life moments when all our masks fall away, and you are just fully present soul to soul. I am the grateful recipient of powerful life lessons learned vicariously as I was privileged to walk alongside others going through every conceivable life scenario. These experiences led me to several more years of schooling, earning an undergraduate degree in philosophy and religious studies at Virginia Wesleyan College, as I wondered about the impact of thought and spirit on life experience.

At the same time I was witness to the growing dysfunction of our health care system. A century ago hospitals had very little to offer beyond care and compassion. Most were started by religious organizations whose tenets included caring for the sick. Over time as both pharmacology and technology developed, health care revolved more and more around drugs and technologies, and care and compassion were more and more marginalized. Finally evolving into 'managed' care, healthcare became another industry reconstructed around a business model whose bottom line was always economic. While most medical professionals still go into these professions from a desire to help and care, the current system makes that functionally impossible much of the time.

Simultaneously in my clinical years in the hospital, as I was becoming ever more disheartened with administrative policies degrading my ability to provide real care to patients, another reality gradually grew into my awareness. The correlation of actual physical condition and outcome clearly did not exist. This went against everything we were taught. Yet eventually after too many experiences of patients who lived through physical impossibilities, and ones who did not survive when there was no physical cause of death, I could no longer ignore that life was entirely dependent upon something beyond the physical. Combined with my frustration with the clinical setting, I realized it was time to move on.

Recognizing that mental and emotional factors have a powerful influence, I spent another few years becoming educated and licensed in counseling psychology. As a psychotherapist the focus is on the only three things human beings do, think, feel, and behave. Although we were taught that the first question to ask is, "How do you feel?" the real focus quickly turned to behavior and thinking. Early in the emergence of psychology during the twentieth century, the emphasis was on behavior. The theory was that if you changed a person's behavior their thinking and emotions would follow. The inadequacy of that view to provide healing led to the growing inclusion of thought and brain function as sources of distress and mental illness. Defined as disease and illness, this linked psychology and medicine, and soon it too became a part of the managed care industry. Currently CBT, or cognitive behavioral therapy, remains the recognized and compensated treatment of choice, supplemented heavily with drug therapy, despite its obvious failure to provide lasting change and healing. Newer therapies arising from the understanding of life as an energy system are strongly resisted by the professional establishment which makes every effort to discredit them, much as they do with holistic vibrational modalities in general.

The spiritual is left entirely out of the process under the misguided thinking that everything spiritual is religious, and that the invisible is irrelevant. With the separation of church and state held as a foundational part of our social culture, ethical codes forbid any spiritual inclusion in the fear that the therapist might impose their own religious bias on their patients. It ignores that at essence every person is spiritual, whether or not they are religious, and even questions the reality of spirit. Worse yet, it ignores the reality that our beliefs always provide the context through which we interpret life events and search for meaning. The baseline of healing is totally missing. There was no way to participate in this system with integrity.

Opting out of the insurance provider option as one I could not ethically engage in, necessitated that my professional work had to be in private practice. While still living in Virginia Beach, I created a new model of professional psychotherapy offered on a fee for service basis in a spiritual setting that allowed me to include the integration of spiritual components along with the mental and emotional ones. This whole person system was so well received it was continued by others after I moved from the area.

After moving back to Pennsylvania where we are originally from, both for my husband's job and so we could be of assistance to our parents in their later years, an unexpected confluence of events presented me with yet another growth spurt. A combination of health and family situations prevented my full scale focus on building my private practice, and during this period several personal experiences and a lot of reading heightened my spiritual focus even more. Along the way I learned of Holos University, where energy medicine and spiritual healing pioneers like Dr. C Norman Shealy, Caroline Myss, Ann and Bob Nunley and others were integrating spiritual, mental, and physical health and providing the needed research that would demonstrate the efficacy of energy modalities. So in 2003, I once again returned to the classroom, spending three more years earning my doctoral degrees and in the process doing research that demonstrated an energetic connection between persons that significantly altered physical, mental, and emotional states. I called it The Heart Field Effect©. Most interesting of all, it was completely independent of any therapeutic technique or process altogether. Just being in the presence of a grounded, centered person whose compassion was focused on you altered your state of being, it changed your experience. The implications of this are astounding, yet so far out of the range of our present mindset that they don't even register.

Long before, from the very beginning of my counseling work, Spirit had instructed me to call my practice, Center for True Self. I had no concept at all of what that meant exactly or how accurate it was in predicting the heart as the goal of my integrative quest. It was the first of many synchronicities that decades later led me to synchronize and organize all that I had learned into a single model of whole person health and wellness. This model honors our own inner wisdom and integrates all the dimensions of our being into an experience of life that is abundant at every level. It is directed by our own attention and intention into who we truly are, ably discovering and fulfilling our own purpose and contributing to our collective evolution.

My purpose in developing the Heart Centered Wellness™ model was not to provide more new information or yet another technique, we have an abundance of both. It was to collate and translate the myriad sources of truth already present into something we can understand and use. It was to create a comprehensive framework that shows how all our human dimensions interact together as a unified whole, and to offer practical ways to apply those principles in daily life.

Many years ago one of my favorite graduate school professors, Dr. Gary Moon, would often use the phrase, 'nothing could be more true or less helpful,' to make the point that no matter how profound or true something is, if we don't see its relevance to our life or situation, or if we don't know how to apply it, it is of no use to us at all. Heart Centered Wellness is designed to provide enough information to see the relevance of our Heart Field to our experience of life, combined with simple tools with which to apply it in the different areas of our lives. It is grounded in the belief that Wellness is a spiritual state. It manifests in coherence and integration of all levels of life in our actual lived experience, and in our conscious ability to navigate and direct life energy from the vibrational center of our heart. The primary access to heart consciousness is a regular practice of Heart Centered Meditation.

Heart Centered Wellness™ (HCW) is a (w)holistic prevention and wellness healthcare model based in the concept that wellness is a spiritual state of positive and abundant living. It is our natural state; always inherent and resuming when obstructions or disconnections are resolved. It recognizes body, mind, and spiritual dimensions of human being and offers information and practices promoting integration into a coherent whole.

Based on an understanding of human beings as energy, light, and information functioning according to universal principles of [Quantum mechanics] vibration and resonance, HCW uses a holistic perspective and a variety of natural modalities to assess and balance energy flow within and between the interdependent aspects of our being, with others and with our environment. Attention to the heart as the vibrational source of human function is central. It initiates, regulates, and coordinates all aspects of life. Key to all HCW is learning how to become consciously aware of your heart and attuned to the information it constantly provides, and ultimately learning to direct its power with focused intention.

A health rather than disease model, HCW incorporates a positive focus on response-ability, and personal strengths as the foundation of life style choices and intentional living. Drug and technology free, this comprehensive approach evaluates each level from your unique perspective, recognizing you are the expert and healer of your life. It focuses on providing the underlying energetic principles combined with practices that allow you to integrate them into daily life in a practical ways. A Heart Centered Wellness™ facilitator can help assess the state and function of physical, mental, and spiritual levels of living and also the communication and balance among them, but only you effect the healing. Your life purpose is considered the overarching context within which each dimension is viewed. Emotion is recognized as the domain of the heart, and feelings as energetic signals of energy flow or obstruction.

Heart Centered Wellness is cross referenced at mind, body, and spiritual dimensions, providing a link between activities of application and the energy affect engendered. It correlates particular experiences with recognized stages of spiritual development, not as a linear or hierarchical ladder, but as a dynamic reference to a spiritual hierarchy understood as a hierarchy of roles rather than superiority or status; all being equally valued and needed within the function of the whole. Heart Centered Wellness doesn't look at the individual in isolation, but includes connections and relationships with others and the environment, recognizing their energy interactions impact our experience in real ways.

An overview of key points we have covered so far summarizes Heart Centered Wellness principles and practices, and correlates them with stages of spiritual development:

At the physical level HCW looks at the structural needs and balance of motion, rest, fuel, and environment.

At the mental level, the balance of left/right brain, hypo/hyper-activity, and stimulation for growth are considered. Head/heart communication, balance and self-talk reveal the sense of separation or union with aspects of self, others, and our world.

At the level of spirit, experience, perspective, awareness, interest, and activity provide the context of meaning or values which determine your perceptions and evaluation of life experiences. Increasing resilience and inner peace resulting from internal motivation and intentional choice allows you to direct your life energy and affect your environments, both internal and external.

Key elements and useful practices in each of the life domains:

Physical- *"Life in the heart begins when consciousness is centered in feeling."*   Hazrat Inayat Khan

- Practice of Heart Centered Meditation leading to a physical state of coherence
- Energy exercises and movement to clear/connect chakras and balance your energy field
- Breath practices; complete breaths, 4 element breathing

- Grounding; nature, earthing
- Water; our basic body resonance faculty. ½ body wt. in oz., blue bottle water
- Fuel (food); Real, non-GMO, locally grown and in season.
- Rest: 6-8 hrs. 90 min. cycles, over time meditation decreases sleep need.
- Movement: any kind, just move most of awake time.
- Body types (Aryuvedic) with different requirements; Kapha, Pitta, Vata

Mentwbar – *"The mind is the servant of the heart."* Hazrat Inayat Khan

- Focus: from outside to inside. Heart Centered Meditation develops concentration and contemplation.
- Stress Response=fear perception, cortisol cascade leading to fight, flight, freeze response; leads to inflammation (precursor to all chronic disease); immediately decreases immune system by 50%, chronic stress kills brain cells.
- EFT and WHEE; tapping/narrative techniques to disconnect stress patterns from self-worth; Dan Benor
- Eden exercises to balance adrenal glands and stress hormones; Donna Eden
- Autogenic training (90 Days to Stress Free Living); Norman Shealy
- Inspirational reading, music, sound, color to alter mental state
- T'aiji and QiGong: mental direction and control of life energy.
- Use of sound to vibrationally alter brain function. Attunement.

- Attention/Intention/Expectation- mental activities that shape perception/attitude/interpretation.
- Effects of meditation on emotion, cognition, perception, memory.

Emotional- *"Every moment of every day, what you feel in your heart is a command in the Mind of God."*
                                    -Gregg Braden

- Heart level awareness. Heart Centered Meditation.
- "Be still and know that I am God."
- 'Ah' sound, musical note 'Fa'
- Gestational role of Darkness: the field of infinite possibilities, Black Madonna, dark energy/matter that makes up 99% of the universe, feminine aspect of the divine.
- Buddhist emotional types; grasping/fear, rejecting/anger, denial/adrift.
- Ho'oponopono – healing from the place of unity, the Heart Field Effect©.
- Emotional Habits of healthy people: Savoring the moment, non-judgment, self-awareness, accepting limitations of self and others, remembering joyful moments, optimism, connecting, resolving conflicts, having fun, relaxing habits, sharing gratitude and love, living an authentic and meaningful life.

Spiritual – *"You are not a drop in the ocean, you are an ocean in a drop."* The level of universality.

- Wholeness, holy, holistic, holon, holographic, all terms defining the presence of the whole in each part.
- Torus or toroidal describe flow of life energy in humans and all life; characteristics include an open system that, while discrete, also takes in and gives out energy.
- Heart Centered Meditation provides a means of expanding your conscious awareness beyond mindfulness and thought to the energy level of feeling and emotion in the heart.
- Resistance to change is the key obstacle to spiritual development. Willingness to change the only requirement.
- Embodied Spirit= goal of human life. To BE Love in action in the world.

Dimensions of Heart Centered Wellness: Focuses and Features:

Stage One:
Physical/Mental
Relaxation Response
The Physical Heart
Attention: Choosing focus
Bio-feedback/Autogenic Training/Autonomic self-regulation
Physiology of Heart Centered Wellness: decreased BP, cortisol levels, stress, inflammation, chronic illness; increased grounding

Stage Two:
Mental/Emotional
Developing Resilience
The Emotional Heart
Intention
Entangled Minds
Shifting from head to heart
Mental/Affective effects: increased calm, peacefulness, self-control, integration of inner/outer experience

Stage Three:
Emotional/Spiritual
Wellness/Abundant Living
The Spiritual Heart
Expansive perspective
Unitive Consciousness

Features:

Stage One	Stage Two	Stage Three
Posture	Concentration	Contemplation
Breath	Directed Breath	Being Breath
Visualize	Meditate	Unitive Experience
Awareness	Heart	Collective
Knowing	Consciousness	Conscious
Response-able self	Feeling	Being
Gratitude	Whole Self	True Self
	Forgiveness	Compassion/Loving Kindness

The Heart Centered Wellness approach is not only comprehensive, but also negates a 'one right answer' or 'one size fits all' way of integrating wellness, making it clear that context matters. It honors the cyclical nature of life and the importance of locating where you are in the particular cycle you want to address; for instance of recognizing whether expansion or contraction is more useful in the particular moment or situation.

The importance of replacing either/or thinking with the more holistic both/and worldview allows us to see both the positive and negative realities associated with a particular choice or view, and keeps the whole in view rather than just one side of it. Heart Centered Wellness returns us to wholeness (holiness) by locating and integrating all aspects of being into a synchronized coherent harmony that allows for all dimensional energies to function effectively. It defines wellness as a spiritual state of harmonic integration into a larger context than your individual self, and makes life a continuous process of keeping your attention on the presence of our essential
True Self.

10 HEART CENTERED WELLNESS: THE PERSONAL

"...the most direct route to cosmic resonance is to awaken your heart, which has a more profound intelligence than your mind."
Barbara Hand Clow

Personal transformation is the necessary prerequisite to all other transformation. Although we all tend to focus outward and wish we could change things and others in ways that seem to us would be beneficial, as Gandhi reminded us, we must be the change we wish to see. The good news is that while true that the only one we can change is our self, it's equally true that it is all any of us can do, and it is all that is needed. To do it in alignment with the master plan of the Divine, we need to understand who and what we are. As we are attuned we see our self, the world and others differently, we feel different and our e-motion sends entirely different frequencies of energy radiating into the inner and outer environments. That changes everything.

Someone once poetically put it that we are like an art project. God gives us the gift of life, and what we make with it is our gift back to God. If we don't understand the properties of our art supplies and how to use them to create most effectively, it's unlikely that the finished product will be what we dreamed of creating. The reality is that you are so a part of the world that your slightest action contributes to its reality. Everything you think, feel, and do changes the atmosphere and the lives of others. We are all singing in life's choir, and there is no lead. No one is more important than another. Whether our voice is loud or soft it is the same Divine music. We are one melody, and one heart. We are each a hologram and a fractal in the much larger hologram.

Humanity is on the verge of whole new ways of seeing and understanding ourselves. Primary among them is seeing separation as false. Following close behind is the shift from seeing human life as physical matter operating through biochemistry and molecular means, to the underlying energy reality that we are energy and function vibrationally within frequency ranges that are dynamic and constantly adjusting to coordinate and regulate our many functions and dimensions.

At the center of you is your own unique vibrational signature and drumbeat; your heart. Beating as early as four weeks after conception, it initiates, regulates, differentiates, and communicates with every cell of our being in a coherent and synchronizing role. It's like the symphony conductor. It receives and transmits untold frequency messages carrying coded information both within and without your body, mind, and spirit, orchestrating on a moment by moment basis the symphony of your life. Unlike your brain, which can be nonfunctional for long periods of time while life still goes on, when your heart stops beating for just a few minutes your life here is over. It's not that everything stops; it doesn't. It's that the master vibrational frequency transmitter and receiver is no longer coordinating messages to and from all the parts and dimensions that make up the whole of you. The intersection of the different planes of body, mind, and spirit is within our heart. When the conductor steps off the podium, the music stops. All of our spiritual traditions have long recognized the centrality of the heart. It is indeed strange that our allopathic medicine is still enamored with the brain and looks at the heart in such a limited way.

We each get to know our heart and its power through the inner attention, sensations and feeling arising in the practice of meditation. As we become conscious of our heartbeat, we are starting to tune in, to expand our conscious awareness beyond the plane of brain and thought. It still includes all that was before, it's just more. As we cultivate the capacity to stay present with whatever feeling presents itself, the false self of ego resists, presenting us with a cacophony of thoughts, reasons why we shouldn't do this. This is dumb. Nothing is happening, I'm wasting my time. I must be doing it wrong. I don't feel anything. Anything to make us stop what feels dangerous and threatening to the false self of our ego.

Heart Centered Wellness provides an interpretive lens of energy principles and particular life engaging practices that, used consistently, allow us to become more and more conscious of our feelings—our energy messages—and our heart. Perhaps even more important, it connects what we already know as many separate things into one coherent reality within a larger picture. As we become heart conscious, our false self ceases to exist as our True Self is experienced, recognizing our spiritual essence and living out of this much larger context.

We have covered the basics of Heart Centered Wellness. Personal application is typically where we run into snags, get frustrated, and often just give up. So let's look at a couple of common experiences and misconceptions that can get in the way, and some additional tools that can boost our experience of living from our heart.

One of the difficulties we have is that we make everything so difficult. Getting to know your own Heart Field is not difficult. It is your natural state. It may feel strange at first because it really does completely reorient us. Remember we said earlier mankind has spent the last several thousands of years developing the mental realm of thought and thinking. We have already entered a new age about which we'll say more later, but here our focus is on the personal. Let's acknowledge that we're talking about a complete reorientation of our way of being in the world. It's not just a tinkering around the edges. It shifts everything.

We are just at the point of taking the first steps. And just like when we learned to walk as little ones, our first steps are wobbly and we fall down a lot. Like a toddler learning to walk, we don't berate our self, say we just can't do it, and give up. Learn from them. Just laugh, get up and start again. There is an inner drive that propels us if we approach it playfully. We just keep at it and gradually we gain strength and balance in this new heartful way of being and navigating in the world.

As humanity is now taking its first baby steps in this new arena of life, all that each of us do contributes to it or resists it. We each only have to attend to our own self. We don't have to go out there and convince everyone else to change. We just have to change us. It's really all we have to do. Interestingly, as we change, it changes everything and everyone around us as well.

We don't have to figure it all out first. We can't. We don't know what all is coming, what exactly it will look like. But we can, and do need to take the little steps every day that reorient us and take us in a different direction. The first change of direction is from outward to inward. This means making a priority of taking care of self first. This flies in the face of all we have been taught. It is not selfish, it is essential. In a very real sense, we cannot love others any more than we love ourselves. Love one another AS you love yourself, is a statement of fact. It's all that's possible. It doesn't mean that you suddenly become self-absorbed and no longer care for others. It means that you must first do your own work, before you are equipped to serve anyone else. You can't offer a True Self you don't yet know. In a very real way, you cannot serve others unless you first serve yourself. Like the airline instructions say, put on your own mask first. Be gentle with yourself, but make a firm commitment to honor your heart's instruction by both listening to it, and acting on what you hear.

Approaching this whole thing playfully will serve you much better than being too serious about it. Remember, this is your natural state you are returning to, so it's already there inside you. You are just getting the obstacles out of the way to uncover, to re-cognize it, to re-member it.

The process needed is different for males and females, although the goal is the same. We are all switching our orientation, but there are different processes that we need to go through to get there. The last age of mental focus focused on factors of the masculine principle of action, the linear step by step binary electric function of the brain, and so it was a natural fit to males. The new age we have entered expands to the heart. It is aligned with the feminine principle of wholeness, receptivity, and magnetic attraction. It is holistic and holographic by nature rather than linear, and females find it a natural fit that aligns with their organic experience. Just like different body types require different things to be healthy and balanced, males and females have different tasks needed at this time to develop their awareness and learning to skillfully navigate their Heart Field.

The first step for males is the really big one of re-defining what feelings and emotion are. It's no secret that for generations men have been taught that this whole arena of human experience is 'girly', weak, silly, not important, and needed to be controlled and largely ignored and overcome. Realizing that feelings and emotion are actually critical energy messages is the first step, but don't expect that recognizing that fact will suddenly turn a switch and you can just start embracing and treasuring your feelings. It might work that way for a few, but for most, overcoming many generations of this way of thinking will take many 'falls and getting back up' to change. It is not, though, out of your nature.

All little boys start out able to cry and express their feelings easily just as girls do, so it's in there. It's just that you have a lot more social conditioning to undo. And so getting in touch with your feelings, befriending them, is a great place to start.

How do you do this? First is giving yourself permission. That may sound silly, but it's not. You may have to keep an affirmation that feelings are message, emotions are sensing energy in motion in your head or pocket to pull out and repeat each time you find yourself reverting to old thinking. An easy way to start is to heighten your awareness of body sensations. When you have a feeling, notice where you feel it in your body. What sensations do you have? How would you describe it? As you do this over and over, you gradually bring feeling more and more into your conscious awareness. When you are feeling emotion do the same thing, and also notice what thoughts are attached to the feeling. Begin to develop a sense of gratitude toward your feelings. These simple steps will take you a long way toward reconnecting with your feelings. And because feelings are the language of the heart, you are becoming more conscious of heart mind at the same time.

Another thing you can do is recognize that you can release the need for control. You no longer have to fix everything. You don't have to be in charge. This can be a great relief. It's not all up to you anymore. In fact, you can now give yourself permission to follow rather than always being expected to lead. It doesn't make you less, or less powerful in any way. It's just a change of role, and all roles are needed equally in the healthy function of the whole. This is a hard sell in linear thinking where hierarchy means superior and inferior, higher and lower. In fact it can't be authentically done mentally for exactly this reason. In meditation as your heart mind consciousness emerges you discover that spiritual hierarchy is not linear. It's about different roles, not rank. The heart is not linear, it pulses, flows, radiates, but does not go in straight lines. Living from the heart is a different experience all together.

It means you have to look at your view of females. In this new age of the heart, it is their natural domain, and they will necessarily be its leaders. This is not about giving up power. It is about power of a different sort. In this light, we need to completely rethink what power actually is and how it works. We live in a world where we have been taught that power is might, force, bigger, faster, being strongest against 'others' that are seen because of their differences as hostile and threatening. Defense is the proper word. You have been told that all these defenses are a sign of strength, when in actuality we all know defense is what is needed when we feel weak, unsafe, under attack, and need to protect ourselves. Defense is not strength, it is usually a sign of weakness and sense of separation. Bruce Lipton pointed out this very process at the level of the cell; it is always in either a growth or defense mode. When in defense it can't grow. It is the same process at the level of the person.

We need to recognize violence for what it most often is, failure to have an effective way to respond. Bullying either on the playground or battlefield is always at its foundation a sign of fear and weakness. Fear is the false 'out of heart' experience of lacking love. It doesn't display power. In fact, it is just the opposite. It comes out of a sense of separation that is false. To not defend does not equate with 'doing nothing,' the common rejoinder when someone is still stuck in the either/or framework of binary thinking or a victim mentality. It takes the deeper and higher consciousness of the heart to see it from a different perspective. It moves us from the inauthentic power of the false self to authentic power of True Self.

To know our True Self, our false self must die. This is what is behind the many spiritual injunctions to 'die before you die,' and Jesus' statement, 'unless I go, the Spirit cannot come.' Our false self is our over-defended ego, and it must be transformed for the True Self to be revealed. Until it is, it continually gets in the way and obstructs our every effort to be real. Richard Rohr says it this way, "Anything less than the death of the false self is useless religion."

For females the initial task of being aware at the heart level is somewhat easier. Feelings and emotion have always been our natural domain. We naturally experience the whole, and are aware of the importance of connection and relationships. The spiritual realm is familiar to us, and we automatically group together as an organic need. Our roles as birth givers, nurturers, and care givers provide many experiences of connection and interdependence, and belie separation as a reality. We do things collectively all the time. Our dilemma comes not from disconnection to our heart, but rather from the dissonance between what our hearts feel and an external world of materialism presents as real. We have always realized that our happiness and joy are in the shared experiences of life. We have the inner conflict of our actual experience with what a male dominated world defines. We have too often believed it rather than what our hearts told us.

For us, the challenge is to own the power of the feminine. While that may sound like we would embrace it enthusiastically, it's rarely so. The initial experience can be terrifying. We are so much more powerful than we ever knew, that our early encounters with it can feel overwhelming. It also goes against the cultural grain of how we have been taught to see ourselves and our roles in life as much as it does for males. We were taught to be subservient, to please people, and to take care of others first. The primary things we were valued for were physical. In the mental and spiritual institutions of culture we are the last to have a seat at the table of power.

Early efforts at feminine power and leadership were often strident. Engulfed in the same prevalent cultural viewpoint, women tried to project power by expressing it in masculine ways. Other women perhaps fearing their own subconscious reality, were often the harshest critics. There have certainly always been some women who do live from their hearts, and we are becoming more and more numerous. We too need to understand our feelings as the messages they are. Rather than controlling them or letting them control us, we need to honor them with our attention and gratitude. As we become empowered and inner directed by our heart, self-confidence is generated and we become undeterred by external factors. This is true power, a very different experience than the false control of trying to manipulate the external environment.

Just as our brain is the functional masculine principle in our body, the heart is the feminine principle. The sacred marriage of both is needed for our full human experience. Our immediate task is to connect as fully and consciously with our hearts as we have with our brains. Just as we addressed the value of asking a better question earlier, we notice that the brain and heart ask different questions. The brain asks, what pattern does this fit? The heart asks, is this true, loving, and helpful? One leads to reaction and repeating old patterns, the other invites us to respond creatively in ways that serve higher goals. Women who are naturally attuned to this dimension must first trust it, and then lead the way. And men must be willing to follow. It is a major shift that will call all of us to new thinking, feeling, and behavior. Our roles, our institutions, and our cultures will all be dramatically altered as we grow into our True Selves collectively, and the Noosphere becomes the experienced reality for everyone. For all of us, male and female alike, the old cliché is true, what you see is what you get. The question is which eyes are you using? What reality do you choose to see? That is the one you are creating.

There are signposts along the way to help us determine where we are on the path, and tools which can assist in our growing Heart Field awareness. We have gone over a number of them. In fact, there are many, many threads of science and spirit which address these same realities in much greater detail, and I have tried to include enough specific references that those of you who want more detailed understanding have a place to start. What has been missing is a link that helps us weave the individual threads into whole cloth, to see the connections and relationships of the bigger picture in a way that we see why they matter to us, and offers specific ways to implement them within our daily lives. That is the main purpose of this book.

The search for God is really the same search as finding our True Self. As we learn to concentrate our mind and direct it to the contemplation of our heart, our consciousness expands to the awareness of the presence of our spirit—of all Spirit—and we are guided with the trustworthy 'still small voice' of our intuitive heart. Jung said, "The knowledge of the heart is in no book and is not to be found in the mouth of any teacher, but grows out of you like the green seed from the dark Earth." As we make our choices and choose our actions from the heart our experience of life is altered significantly.

When we are learning a new skill or language it is always awkward at first, and helpful to have some signposts or markers to see where we are. Gradually as you gain trust in yourself you no longer need them, but initially they are reassuring. Each of us is a part of an evolutionary leap taking place within humanity. We are being transformed. Having some sense of key concepts that are related to our experience of this and some practices that assist our attunement to it can ease the chaos and confusion that always accompanies the new, and helps us see that there is a path beneath our feet.

I like a Lakota prayer that says this so much more poetically:

Teach me how to trust my heart,

My mind, my intuition, my inner knowing,

The senses of my body,

The blessings of my spirit.

Teach me to trust these things

So that I may enter my sacred space

And love beyond my fear

And thus walk in balance

With the passing of each glorious sun.

The simplest of psychological and energy principles is that what we give attention to expands. Like all profound things this sounds so simple that we forget to apply it. When we are not consciously directing our mind, it is attracted to every passing object, thought, and whatever is loudest or shiniest in the moment. The rapid increase of Attention Deficit Disorder in our culture correlates to the increasing speed and volume of information and activity going on around us. When we are not consciously directing our mind and focusing our thoughts they just wander. Persons with higher sensitivity and higher intelligence tend to wander more easily. ADD and ADHD are not pathological, they are energetic, and respond much more readily to energy focusing modalities than pharmacological ones. We have said, what we see is what we get. Perhaps we should add, choose carefully. If we give our attention to the positive, it expands through the life energy our attention provides. If we give our attention to the negative the same thing happens. Both are always really present. Which one do you choose to grow?

A second energy concept I have stated is that Wellness is a spiritual state. Why is this so? Because the level of health we are able to experience is limited by our ability to consciously choose within that domain. All of the dimensions that make up the whole of us are operational all the time. They all have a default program, but we are only able to use our free will or power of choice to the extent we are able to be consciously aware in that domain. We can be physically healthy by providing for the physical needs of our bodies. We can be mentally healthy by feeding, using, and exercising our minds. We can be emotionally healthy by keeping our energy fields clear, unobstructed with unhealed traumas in the fluid layers, and disconnections in the structured layers that leak energy and allow outside energies to intrude. To be spiritually healthy requires the death of our false self and experience of our True Self. That is the journey of our lives, finding out who we are and why we are here.

There are stages of wellness. They too of course are dynamic and not fixed, so we experience them all at some moments, while residing predominantly at a particular level. Probably most of us are focused mainly on the first two stages, prevention and healing. Prevention includes both doing the things that support health and staying away from things and situations that threaten it. Healing is a huge need and area of interest at this current time. Partially it is personal and related to our lack of understanding of ourselves as energy beings, resulting in diagnoses and treatments that are often not effective and can even complicate the situation further with unintended consequences. The other is a result of the time we live in. As humanity is in the midst of an evolutionary leap, all the unprocessed, unhealed traumas both personal and of our lineages are surfacing in order to be healed so we are able to move forward.

Wellness is significantly more, however, than the absence of disease. As the various dimensions of our being are operating harmoniously we call that coherence. Coherence is not only within each level but also between the levels. It is a state that allows for the growth mode to be operational, and we experience that as thriving—the third stage of wellness. In it we experience joy in activities, our creativity is stimulated mentally, and our inner state is grounded and peaceful. We experience movement forward in life and have a sense of anticipation of what is still before us.

Abundant living, the fourth stage, is of course the spiritual promise and our intended ultimate state of human life. It can only be realized as our True Self. It remembers our union with the Divine and lives out of that heart knowledge as a co-creator. It is the experience of our self as Love expressing in the world, and puts us in a state of joy. Peace, love, and joy are the trinity of spiritual wholeness.

In Part II, we listed some specific aspects and practices in each dimension that affect its integrity. Heart Centered Meditation was noted as the one essential that provides the expansion of our conscious awareness beyond the mental mind to the intersection in our heart of all levels of our being. At Holos University Graduate Seminary, I teach an entire semester course on the details and practice development of Heart Centered Meditation along with the emerging physics and quantum science that supports it. It's not practical or necessary here to go into that level of detail, but I do want to provide a little more background on my experience with it and some additional resources for those readers who may want them.

Over a decade ago, shortly after I had finished my research on the Heart Field Effect© and doctoral studies on Energy Medicine and Spiritual Healing, I was considering the need to create specific practical ways to help others connect with their Heart Field energy. The universe in one of those great synchronicities that demonstrate true abundance and provision of our needs had another plan. I was attending the annual Subtle Energy Medicine conference (ISSSEEM) in Boulder, CO. In the bookstore I bumped into Puran Bair, co-author of Living from the Heart. He and his wife Susanna were also attending the conference and presenting a breakout session on a meditation practice they had developed called Heart Rhythm Meditation. The commonality of the same last name and our mutual professional and spiritual focus on the heart was more than enough to start an animated conversation. That was the beginning of a long and fruitful association and deep friendship that continues to this day.

Susanna and Puran were students of Pir Vilayat Khan for many years, studying the teachings of his father, Hazrat Inayat Khan, the great Sufi mystic. Pir Vilayat sent them out with a specific injunction to translate Sufi teachings and practices into ones accessible to the Western mind and culture. They developed "Heart Rhythm Practice to use the mind-body connection to approach the sacred heart through concentration on the physical heart." With this foundation, over time they worked out multiple practical exercises that assist in connecting to the heart, as well as perpetuate this particular lineage. Eventually these practices coalesced into an entire two year program that is now known as the University of the Heart.

Although my work focuses beyond any particular lineage or spiritual master, knowing the Divine is universal, many of their insights and practices are very helpful, and I often recommend their books and practices. I honor and acknowledge their many contributions to the work of the heart, and appreciate deeply their untiring efforts to bring forward the central importance of heart consciousness to so many. A decade ago there were not very many of us doing that. Now there are more and more each day. Heart Field awareness is noticeably increasing post shift, and I expect in the near future it will be the self-evident reality for everyone.

In addition to meditation there are other modalities that can be useful in connecting with our Heart Field energetically. They bypass our mental perceptual grid and defenses by using our other senses and direct energy entrainment to connect, attune, align, and enact at-one-ment.

Sound provides a very powerful influence both through tone and rhythm. Music is the most known to all of us. We all know the mood altering influence of background music, and now our customized play lists provide instant calming or uplifting options that effectively shift our energy. Emoto's water crystal photographs documented the effect of music on water. Since we are largely water, it's not too much of a leap to presume a similar effect in us. The rhythm of the beat as well as the tone of the notes provide very specific effects on our energy fields. Using music is a simple way to instantly alter our energy and our mood.

Spiritual traditions all utilize some forms of rhythm and sound to entrain group cohesion and imprint teachings at a deeper level than words alone can. In addition to music, there is drumming, chanting, toning, singing bowls and crystal bowls. Some traditions use the repetition of sacred names and words to invoke particular qualities. Mantras work similarly. It's believed that the words in pre-modern languages actually created the sound pattern of the quality of Divinity desired, thus energetically attracting its presence.

In holistic health practices all of these things are used with intention to bring about specific energy changes. Each chakra has its own note within the octave that is particular to its function. Affirmations are the modern versions of this. My friend and colleague Gary Malkin, whose first language is music, has extended this very effectively in creating a simple process in which a person first creates their own statement of True Self, then attaches a rhythm to it, and finally adds a melody that accurately expresses its intention. Marrying all three, then adding repetition and volume variation produces a profound healing effect immediately experienced as more authentic self. It's fun to play around with toning and sound and see how it makes you feel.

Light is the other major external source of energy alteration. Sunlight is the simplest and most powerful full spectrum light source. Spending an hour a day outdoors is the easiest and most reliable way to balance your entire Heart Field and synchronize with the Earth. Our resonant frequencies are even harmonic. Earth's heartbeat is known as the Schuman Resonance and averages 7.83Hz. This is found in the ELF, or extremely low frequency, part of Earth's electromagnetic field. This is a carrier wave for 'consciousness at rest' in the human; half way between Theta (4-8cps) and Alpha (8-13 cps) brain waves present in deep but alert relaxation and intuitive attunement which opens portals of consciousness to expanded awareness into realms beyond the physical. You may have noticed that when you spend more time outdoors you feel more grounded, relaxed, and energized.

Light is the visible, but not yet particularized realm between the patterns in sound that are not visible and the expression manifest when the light is organized into a particular form or hologram that we see as matter. When we pay attention we can often notice light in some in-between states, like orbs, or in the auras of trees or humans. It's another example of attention expanding our awareness. Humans in general have not been aware of this for some time, and so our perceptual ability has atrophied. You may not even know you have this ability, but it is present in all of us and can be developed just like we develop our muscles by working out. Dr Melinda Connor has written several excellent books describing biofield basics and learning to see auras, and offers workshops and individual instruction that teach this skill in surprisingly short order.

Smell is also a powerful energy stimulant, and aromatherapy and essential oils used properly can be very effective adjuncts to balancing our energy in specific ways. These are very popular right now, and so a note of caution is needed. Essential oils are only as good as the ingredients and the process that produced them. The commercial market and practitioners that lack in depth knowledge have exploded onto the holistic scene, and so it is good to check your source. Improperly or synthetically produced oils are not at all the same thing vibrationally.

Crystals have also become very popular over the past several decades. Ancient in use, spiritual and holistic healers have always recognized their ability to store, remove, attract and direct energy related to their particular structure. Like water, crystals can store energy patterns which, placed in your field can entrain the similar patterns of crystalline structures within your body.

Overall, knowing how each of these things and the ones covered earlier in the book relates energetically to your own Heart Field allows you to be a much more intentional co-creator and artist of your life. It's not that you have to do a bunch of new things in an already busy life. It often reveals a need to simplify and get back to the basics. It is a basic shift from outer to inner awareness. As we are completely re-orienting our viewpoint to that of energy, feeling, and Heart Field, new and different knowledge must be married to new choices and actions that reflect the higher understanding it brings us. Less is often more.

We can all observe that lack of understanding of how our life energy works has resulted in some completely unintended consequences. Social justice efforts that fight against some cause are one example. Instead of diminishing or eliminating the injustice, it perpetuates and energetically strengthens the very thing not wanted by directing their own life energy and attention to it. Additionally it amps up the energy from the other side, cumulatively having just the opposite effect of what is desired. Far more productive and aligned with how energy, attention and intention function is to work for something. Although it may sound similar, being against war is an entirely different thing energetically than being for peace.

As Oprah is fond of saying simply, when we know better we do better. Take charge of your own wellness by first knowing who you truly are and what your purpose is. Determine how well you want to be, then know what choices support you in doing that. Making the choices and acting on them, all cumulatively put you in the driver's seat of your life. The mystic painter Rassouli said it well, "I let the eyes of my heart be the watchful vison that guides me to my wellness and wellbeing." May it be so.

We each lead not by what we think, but by our own vibration, intention, and alignment. Be the source of the world you want to live in.

11 HEART CENTERED WELLNESS: THE COLLECTIVE

"Real love is a permanently self-enlarging experience."
   M. Scott Peck

It's not just about you. We all experience ourselves as the center of the universe, which is an energy reality as the apex of every vortex converges to a single point of manifestation. As we notch up the microscope to a higher power we see that we are an integral part of larger and larger wholes.

We are dancing with the stars. No, not the TV show, although I'm a big fan. In the language of energy resonance, we are all dancing with the stars all the time. Interestingly there are a number of similarities. It's a microcosm of what's possible in the macrocosm. We all start with our strengths and weaknesses, preferring most often to show others only the strengths. At some point, no matter how acclaimed we may be, we find ourselves still feeling 'less than.' This may be more a factor of not being known as our whole selves rather than the commonly thought 'not good enough' that therapists frequently work with. Rumi put it well when he said, we rarely hear the inward music, but we're dancing to it none the less.

The brilliance behind DWTS is not the glamorous costumes, the skill of dancing, and so on. It is in watching the courage of persons already well known in some sphere of life other than dancing, publically step out to try something they have not yet done. In contrast to almost every other show in what is called the 'reality' genre, without any manipulation this one creates genuine bonds of support and encouragement. In an atmosphere of mentoring by those skilled in dance it is expected that the professional the stars are paired with will teach and support them; discerning their strengths and choreographing dance sets that build upon them in a way that takes them beyond where they ever thought they could go. In the process their vulnerabilities are inevitably displayed on a very large public stage. What organically occurs with regularity is the support, encouragement, and even love expressed between the contestants and between the stars and the dance professionals.

Although both the dancers and professionals speak of this frequently, I've not heard anyone comment yet on the stark contrast of this organic reaction to the usual reality programs in which the competition engenders secretiveness, manipulation, aggression, and the ubiquitous 'us against them' mentality that is costing humanity so much. It becomes a relevant question to ask, what is the difference? Just as a science fiction book can present us with possibilities we might not consider under the guise of non-fiction, this stark difference might point us to factors that give birth to cooperation, collaboration, and community instead of separation, aggression, and control.

One notable observation that jumps right out is that their differences, rather than separating them became the essential keys to their success. Another is that they all realize they are equally vulnerable and interdependent upon the others. The very vulnerability that we all try so hard to disguise is the bond that we all share. When shared openly it stimulates compassion and connection; just the opposite of what the fears of our false self tell us will happen. When that deep bond of shared vulnerability occurs it also carries with it a permanence. Energetically it is entanglement that exists outside of space/time.

We live in a world that shares many of these same analogies. It's a world that is in the midst of massive evolutionary change; one of the leaps that only occur in thousands or millions of years. The fear factor increases exponentially with change for those who are not yet conscious of their True Self. We see the evidence of this fear both in individuals and groups all around us. So what is going on?

The shift happened. More accurately, it has been happening for some time, but for most there was that highly expectant moment of December 21, 2012, when the Mayan calendar seemed to end, and a Galactic Convergence occurred. While many may have heard that term, few seem to have a clear idea exactly what it was or why it mattered. There are also those skeptics who declared it nonsense. In a nutshell, the galactic convergence was the moment in time when multiple cycles of planets, stars, and galaxies all coincided at the same juncture. As you might guess, because of the vastly different sizes, distances, and lengths of cycle this is a very rare occurrence. It is also difficult to pinpoint in time given the speed variation of the different cycles, and is actually not just one day in Earth time. Since some of the cycles are thousands or millions of years long and others are quite short, it is more accurate to say that the date was the midpoint of all of them. Given what we do know about gravitational pull effects that are the basis of our astrology it is consistent to conclude that such a rare and large occurrence may well bring massive changes to our planet and to each of us.

In the year leading up to it there were wild and widely varying opinions of what might happen; how the future might drastically change or not even exist. From the end of the world, to a pole reversal, and equally speculative views, most only knew it was the end of the Mayan Calendar. When the date came and went without any major Earth shaking occurrence the media and many along with them decided that nothing happened and the whole topic disappeared again from the public square. The status quo was again safe.

A different perspective grounded in multiple cultures and traditions over thousands of years is provided when the spiritual perspective is not dismissed as irrelevant. The fact that the same story has existed over thousands of years in distant locations and in every major group of humans gives us pause. It is especially important for us now because we are living in the days referred to in all of their teachings. As the Hopi say, we are the ones we have been waiting for.

While there have been many different groups aware of what some call the Perennial Philosophy, a common thread is a much larger purview than we normally take in thinking about these things. In spite of many well researched sites and reports of much earlier and more advanced civilizations on the Earth in the distant past, most people are only aware of several thousand years of history at most. In religious traditions historical records typically are only as long as the story of the spiritual master recognized as their leader. In worldly matters they are limited to the beginnings of the particular culture. In both cases the worldview stays small in historical terms.

A higher, deeper, broader, and longer perspective has much to offer. This becomes self-evident if we look beyond a single tradition of any kind. When we do, it quickly becomes apparent that common threads run through all of them along with delightful and colorful differences. As we become familiar with more of them, patterns start to emerge. Then we start to see even bigger patterns that those patterns are part of. They are all telling the same story. A hologram starts to appear as we see the whole reflected in every part.

Throughout this book we have emphasized the importance of wholeness. For humans the whole of life has been considered to be on Earth. Accepted views in every discipline were Earth centric. Even our personal astrological charts revolve around only the planets in our own solar system. In human history it was not that long ago that Galileo was excoriated for suggesting that the Earth revolved around the Sun rather than the other way around. When we see the changes that have taken place in just the last hundred years it is amazing. When over the last few decades our space technologies sent back confirmation that there are not just other solar systems and galaxies, but billions of universes, our minds aren't able to process the implications.

We noted that everything has both positive and negative aspects. Certainly our very recent cyber sphere is a good example. We now have access to a volume of information unthinkable even in our own early life. The rate of new information now doubles so fast that it is humanly impossible to take it in, let alone process it. Yet our cultural institutions and customs lag behind and continue to operate in the same way they did long ago. The resulting social dissonance is predictable. Data warehousing which didn't exist very long ago, is now a huge enterprise. Issues of privacy are being debated through a legal system that itself is antiquated and ill equipped to solve the issue. The whole topic of governments, nation states, immigration, and economic commerce, information rights, and more are being challenged. Those who feel threatened by change fight to hold on to the familiar. Some of the more adventuresome rush full speed ahead without attention or intention to potential consequences. Both have some valid considerations, yet neither are addressing the underlying issue.

We can't move forward from the false self. It is only by going through the transformation to True Self that we are able to realize in our experience who it is we really are, and what our purpose is. It can't be known with our mental rational intellect. It is not irrational, it is transrational. It can only be experienced through an open heart. At the level of the Heart Field this is apparent as we note that it is in the heart that the various dimensions of our being intersect. It's sort of like being in Penn Station in New York City. As the central hub of several vast transit systems that run independently, it's easily possible to get on any of them from here. The heart is also where we connect with others and all that we consider external. When experienced in the heart the sense of individual being dissolves in the unitive realization of our True Self. At the same time the sense of our unique qualities and purpose are also heightened.

Where do you live? When you are asked this question do you automatically respond with a street address? The address where your body resides? This is a different question.

Where do you live?

For most of us, creatures made up of body, mind, and spirit, the answer is, in our heads. You may quickly descent; no, no, look how much attention we give to our bodies. While that may at first appear to be true—many people spend most of their time, attention, and money focused on making their body look a certain way, what cloth to drape it in, or develop their muscles extensively to demonstrate physically superior form, or learn a particular sport so in depth that they can outperform everyone else—still we must ask, who is doing this? They are making these choices from their minds.

Others focus primarily on spirit and would say, "We are spirit just having a human lifetime." Often they will neglect the body, thinking it illusory or unimportant. Some even chastise it or deny its physical needs, from food, sleep to sex, demonstrating disdain for the physical.

Still others focus almost entirely on the mind. Cogito ergo sum, I think therefore I am as Descartes said many years ago. They may focus almost entirely on thought, learning a great deal, considering what others have thought and comparing philosophies looking for what is right. They have decided that the particular level they focus on is most important, and give most of their intentional attention to that sphere of being.

Many less intentional people allow whatever is in their environment determine where their attention goes. Our minds are always moving, thinking. It is where we largely live. Left unattended they just follow whatever is present in the moment. Today that can often be a TV, computer, or earbuds keeping the mind occupied with entertainment while the person remains essentially asleep to what is actually going on within themselves and the larger world.

While it may at first appear that all these folks have nothing in common, in fact they are all doing the same thing—focusing on one aspect of life largely to the exclusion of the others. As holographic, holy, whole beings we are simultaneously all of them. The difference lies in where we place our attention, or perhaps more accurately stated, with how much intention we place our attention.

Our minds are important, but to what extent do we focus them with intention? As people awaken from the sleep of inattention, realize they have choices, and become increasingly intentional, the interconnections become obvious in our experience. When we say we are body, mind, and spirit that is a statement of truth. We are simultaneously ALL of them here in our life on this world. No one part of us is less important than the others. It is not an either/or issue. We need to be aware of and care for all of them as what they are; different dimensions of our whole being. Integrating them into a coherent whole experience and function is what we are here to do.

Increasingly we are becoming aware that the questions of life are not which dimension is the real one, but rather how aware we are of each. Can we expand our conscious awareness to all of them? Previously we have discussed where it is we place our consciousness, in the body, in the mind, or in the spirit. That is the old question. We are in a new time and space. The question for us at this moment is can we live our daily lives integrating conscious experience of all as an integrated whole being? How we answer this question, or even if we ask it, determines our future reality. As beings of energy, it is never IF we have life, for the laws of physics tell us energy cannot be created or destroyed, it can only change form. The question then shifts to what kind of life, or what experience of life do we choose. Before we choose, we have to realize we have a choice.

This first becomes apparent to us in the area of perception. We have all seen the optical illusions that demonstrate how easily our perceptions create the reality we see, and how we are able to shift our seeing to see something entirely different and equally true. Once we realize the importance of perception, its power over the way we experience the world, we also can see that we have choices. We can change what we see by how we look at it. This is not a frivolous game. Once we have tried it, we quickly realize that how we perceive a given situation determines how we feel about it, how we experience it. When we choose to change our perception, not only our perception changes, but so do the choices we make about how to react, what to say, what to do, that ultimately change the experience for all involved. At first this may confuse us; is anything real we ask? But life goes on, things keep happening, and so eventually if we stick with it rather than becoming cynical and relativistic, we realize how powerful we are. By simply changing our perception, we change our experience, and our different choices then change the experience for all. Stories abound of persons who by standing in their truth changed the story for all of us.

As I write this we are in yet another political election cycle where each politician argues for their story of how the world really is and what change is needed to make it a better place. People choose who to elect largely on whose story matches up most closely with their own. In the transition zone between the absolutist view—we are just physical (science), mental (psychology), or spiritual (religion)--and the holistic view that we are all of them at the same time, lies an intermediate zone we call relativity. From this perspective, if nothing is absolute, then everything is just relative. This seems like the only possible conclusion when made from the either/or perspective we have all been entrenched in for a very long time.

As we are awakening to the abundant evidence in life that everything is interconnected and it is all one great whole, we shift into a both/and level of understanding where acknowledging one truth doesn't deny the reality of the other. From this perspective it isn't a question of is this true or that, but this is true and that is true, so what is the connection and relationship? An entirely different world emerges to our senses. One in which we don't have to ask if we belong or are significant; we can understand that every choice made by every person is connected to and affects all others all the time.

Over the past several decades the mind body connection has become increasingly evident. The power of our attitudes and thinking on our body is now generally acknowledged, although for most if something is physical that means it is real, concrete, and only changeable with physical interventions. What has largely been left out is spirit. Ever since the Cartesian dualism emerged several hundred years ago, and science and religion tacitly agreed that they each had authority over different domains, science has described and investigated only physical, objective reality, and spiritual esoteric matters were left to religion to define and supervise. The problem with this of course is that we experience life as a whole. We don't say, my body will go to the doctor today to see about this physical issue, my mind will go to the library to learn something new, and my spirit will go to church, synagogue, or temple to express devotion to my particular god. The destructive results of this fragmentation are all around us. Implicitly we all know this, yet our world continues to teeter along in every sphere of life as though this doesn't exist.

Our understanding of spirit was historically confined to a particular religious viewpoint, most often the one held by our parents or community. In science the invisible world equated with 'not real' even though it acknowledged the effects of forces and fields that undeniably exist by how they influence our physical reality. We have continued the separation of these dimensions of life from the rest. This is especially egregious given that we understand spirit to be the highest level of our being; our energy essence and thereby infinite in its existence. Because religion is considered highly personal and off limits to interference, we have removed it from the public square of inquiry and its influence, although powerful, is ignored. When we can acknowledge the spiritual dimension as ubiquitous and beyond any particular expression of religion it frees us for recognizing that it provides the context of meaning within which we interpret life's experiences. It is that which allows us to redeem suffering by placing it into a larger context of meaning and purpose. It is the heart not the mind that is the place of healing and wholeness.

As our perception grows more and more unitive we realize that it is not only our thoughts and actions that alter external reality. In every moment what we feel is the frequency we are pulsing into the collective where it affects the larger environment. It attracts to us the same frequencies, and alters both the energy of the space we are in and the dynamic pattern of the particular archetype in the collective it connects to. In the twentieth century Jung introduced us to the reality of the collective unconscious. Very rapidly in the twenty first the unconscious is in the process of becoming collectively conscious.

This is the Noosphere; the Earth's own consciousness becoming conscious. Barbara Marx Hubbard is one of the people who has worked for years on the social and cultural aspects of this emerging reality, modeling as well as declaring the feminine leadership needed for its birth. Her model of the Wheel of Co-Creation aligns with that of Kimberly and Foster Gamble's Thrive movie and is based on the twelve social sector circles of life like the medicine wheel, astrological charts, and other models. What Barbara's model adds is the critical identification of the center point of the circle; the twelve plus one reveals the critical addition of consciousness as the connecting factor of all of these domains. Her life models what the divine feminine emerging looks like. After a first half of life birthing and raising children, the second half continues the creativity and nurture as we birth and nurture a whole new humanity.

Charles Eisenstein is another who has given up the easy life of social compliance to explore the communal and social possibilities of authentic human being. After a long season of unpacking the origins of what was broken about the world and questioning what really matters, he set out to define the components of the title of one of his books, The More Beautiful World our Hearts Know is Possible. That journey has led him to his current field of inquiry exploring what the true masculine looks like in complement to the authentic feminine.

Personal consciousness of our True Self is the essential first step for each of us. We cannot give something we do not own. We are each always contributing to the collective in every moment, with every feeling, thought and action. It is only as we are aware at the deep level of the heart that we are able to contribute consciously to the whole with intention. The tipping point of the collective false self dying and awakening to the True Self of collective humanity depends upon sufficient numbers of us having made this journey first within ourselves. We always are and have been co-creating the world with the divine. Like the man who lived his entire life thinking he was poor on his small plot of land, never knowing it was on top of a gold mine, when we are unaware of our heart's riches it distorts our entire reality. Fear based thinking and actions are the inevitable result, with only the brief flashes of peak moments of heart experience that we usually attribute to external persons or setting. Only when we learn to expand our consciousness beyond the mental dimension to the spiritual dimension of the heart intentionally are we able to experience the life of Love that we are, and share that abundance and awareness with others in peace and with joy.

Not too long ago Einstein asked the question, is the universe a friendly place? I would add to that, from where do you choose to get your evidence? The external world presents one view, the internal another. Mind over matter, while a start, is not enough. Mind presents patterns of past experience, the heart presents the present moment pregnant with all of its infinite possibilities. The transformation of the false self to the True Self results from the sacred marriage of the divine with the human; the real meaning of incarnation. There is nothing that is not Love. There are only those who realize this in the experience of heart centered living and see it in every moment, place, and person, and those who are still in the process of awakening.

Connection and relationship instead of separation, both this and that instead of either this or that, are key perceptual components. Heart Centered Meditation is a tool for accessing inner knowing. Recognizing the inner connection of body/mind/spirit makes us attentive to all of them as equally important in the balance of life. It is apparent that neglect of one affects our functional ability in all. Consciously within our heart we follow a way that is beyond the social mainstream; where the cultivation of our essence is a primary value. Our highest goal is not to become more spiritual. That is impossible. At the level of spirit we are and always have been infinitely whole. We too are Love. We are here to embody Spirit in our full humanity as we fulfill our particular role in making heaven on Earth a lived reality.

I'm blessed to have four amazing grandsons, Nick, Sam, Peter, and Fred, who teach me constantly the simple things of what that looks like. When Peter was very young and just learning to talk, he would repeat a phrase that none of us could understand. He patiently repeated it over and over while I kept erroneously guessing its meaning. Finally after many more repetitions than any adult would provide without just giving up in frustration, I got it. He was saying, 'as best you are able,' a phrase included at grace before meals in their family. I believe that it is the same phrase the Divine constantly whispers to each of us in the sanctuary of our deepest heart, never stopping until we get the message.

Know that Love is who you are, and be Love in expression in every moment, as best you are able.

RESOURCE REFERENCE LIST

Claude Swanson, PhD, *The Synchronized Universe, Vol.II, Life Force Energy*

Barbara Marx Hubbard. Social model of co-creators rising.

Desda Zuckerman, *Your Sacred Anatomy*.

Candice Pert,PhD, *Molecules of Emotion*.

Bruce Lipton,PhD, *Biology of Belief*.

Mae-Wan Ho, PhD, *The Rainbow and the Worm*. 2nd ed.

Ervin Lazlo, *The Interconnected Universe*.

Masaru Emoto, *The True Power of Water*.

Gerald H. Pollack, *The Fourth Phase of Water*.

Melinda H. Connor, DD, PhD, AMP, *Advanced Body Reading*.

Caroline Myss, PhD, *Sacred Contracts*.

C. Norman Shealy, MD, PhD, *90 Days to Stress Free Living*.

Charles Eisenstein, *The More Beautiful World our Hearts tell us is Possible.*

Christine Bair, PhD, ThD, The Heart Field Effect, *Advances in Mind-Body Medicine, Winter2008-2009. VOL. 23,NO.4.*

Websites: www.HolosUniversity.org ,

www.HeartCenteredWellness.org

www.ISSSEEM.org

INDEX

ABOUT THE AUTHOR

A mystic and scientist, philosopher and clinician, priestess, prankster, and professor, Christine's passion is weaving the threads of science and spirit into the tapestry of whole cloth. Working with the physical, mental/emotional, and spiritual dimensions of the heart became the stepping stones to consciousness of the Heart Field and the unity of all dimensions of being. Dr. Bair's professional journey began in nursing, continued at Virginia Wesleyan College with a degree in philosophy and religious studies, followed by graduate degrees in counseling psychology and spiritual direction, before culminating in integration in her doctoral work at Holos University. Also ordained, she currently serves on the faculty at HU where she teaches Heart Centered Meditation, and directs the Integrative Health Care track. She resides in Harrisburg, PA, and offers in person and distance counseling and mentoring, as well as workshops, retreats, and Heart Centered Wellness facilitation. Dr. Bair can be contacted at www.HeartCenteredWellness.org or DrChristineBair@gmail.com.

The Heart Field

Christine Bair

The Heart Field

Christine Bair